The Official
SCOTLAND RUGBY YEARBOOK 2003

GreenPark Publishing
151-153 Wick Road, Brislington, Bristol BS4 4HH
Telephone +44(0)117 977 9188
Contact peter@sportspro.co.uk

Published by GreenPark Publishing
Copyright © GreenPark Publishing

All rights reserved.
No part of this publication may be reproduced, stored in a retrieval system, or transmitted, in any form or by any means, electronic, mechanical, photocopying, recording or otherwise, without the prior permission in writing of the publisher.

ISBN 9537 444-1-8

Set in Akzidenz Grotesk by GreenPark Publishing and printed in Great Britain.

CONTENTS

01	Foreword from HRH Princess Anne	4
02	Hall of Fame	5
03	2002 Scrapbook	26
04	The Commonwealth Sevens by Alan Shaw	38
05	Scotland Home of Sevens	41
06	Six Nations Preview by Alan Lorimer	42
07	Barbarians Preview by David Ferguson	48
08	World Cup Preparations by Norman Mair	51
09	Glasgow Rugby by David Kelso	56
10	Borders Contribution by David Ferguson	60
11	Scotland's Place in World Rugby by Todd Blackadder	63
12	Notes from Edinburgh by David Ferguson	66
13	The Rugby Dinner by Frank Moran	70
14	Murrayfield People	72
15	The Return of the Natives by Grahame MacGregor	74
16	Life off the Field by Grant Robbins	78
17	Scotland's Young Bloods by Alan Shaw	81
18	Scotland International referees by George Mackay	86
19	From The Archives	88
20	Scottish Women's Rugby	94
21	McGeechan on Tour by Grant Robbins	98
22	The Calcutta Cup by Alan Evans	101
23	Our Song by David Ferguson	102
24	35 Years of Watching Scotland by Brian Meek	104
25	Matchday Build up by Kevin Ferrie	106
26	Portraits of Redpath as his children see him	112
27	Through the Eyes of a Sassenach by John Scott	113
28	The Impact of Professionalism by Kevin Ferrie	116
29	The Scotland Squad	118

Support makes all the difference

Make it happen

We're delighted to be supporting the RBS Six Nations – just one part of our extensive sports sponsorship programme covering everything from major international events to local competitions for schoolchildren.

The Royal Bank of Scotland

www.rbs.co.uk

01 FOREWARD

BUCKINGHAM PALACE

It gives me very great pleasure to have the opportunity to introduce the first Scotland Yearbook. As a loyal supporter of the Scotland Team I welcome the introduction of such an informative and lively publication. It provides Scotland supporters of all ages with inside knowledge on this season's squad, their performance and preparations for next year's Rugby World Cup in Australia. It also looks back in time and features some of the personalities who shaped Scottish Rugby's past. With features too about the personnel without whom International matches at Murrayfield could not take place and tips on players to watch for the future, new vibrant insight is offered into the world of Scottish Rugby. I hope you enjoy this book and I hope that, like me, you will be at Murrayfield as often as you can for the next chapter in the Scotland Team's history.

Anne

HRH PRINCESS ANNE WITH SCOTLAND CAPTAIN **BRYAN REDPATH** AND **BILL MCLAREN** AT THE OPENING OF THE BILL MCLAREN PRESS GALLERY, MURRAYFIELD

SCOTLAND'S HALL OF FAME

SOME OF THE GREAT PERSONALITIES WHO HAVE ADDED HUGELY TO THE LIFE OF SCOTTISH RUGBY

Gavin Hastings 1986-93

Scott Hastings 1986-97

Andy Irvine 1974-80

John Jeffrey 1986-90

Roy Laidlaw 1980-88

Norman Mair 1951

Ian McGeechan 1974-90

Ian McLauchlan 1969-79

John Rutherford 1979-87

Jim Telfer 1964-70

HASTINGS 1986-93

- Born Edinburgh January 3rd 1962

- Watsonians, Cambridge University, London Scottish, Scotland and British Lions

- Full back in 61 matches, 20 matches as captain of Scotland, Scoring 655 points in total from his Test appearances

- British Lions tours Australia 1989 and New Zealand 1993: 6 Tests

GAVIN HASTINGS has rightly gained a reputation as one of rugby's finest ever full backs. Hastings had all the qualities of a world-class full back; he was reliable with the highball and the touch kick, and was an expert at turning any opponent's attacks around on them. His total Test points score of 655 is a Scottish record. In the 33-6 demolition of England in 1986, he scored eight out of eight kicks, showing his remarkable accuracy and consistent performance under incredible pressure.

HASTINGS 1986-97

- Born Edinburgh December 4th 1964

- Watsonians, Newcastle Northern, Scotland

- Centre / Wing in 65 Test matches, played in same side as his brother in 51 Scotland matches. Scored 10 test tries.

SCOTT HASTINGS making his debut with his brother against France in 1986, Scott Hastings' play was a consistent feature of the Scotland side right up to 1997. He first played for Watsonians at the age of 17, and quickly gained great praise for his powerful attacking running, and ability to break through the seemingly sturdy defensive lines of opposing teams. His tactical defensive play was almost unbeatable, and his regular partnership at centre with Sean Lineen contributed greatly to many Scottish successes, including the 1990 Grand Slam.

IRVINE 1974-80

- Born Edinburgh September 16 1951

- Heriot's FP, Barbarians, Scotland and British Lions

- Full back and wing in 51 matches; scored 10 tries, 25 conversions, 61 penalty goals (273 points)

- British Lions 1974, 1977 & 1980: 9 Tests

ANDY IRVINE was the most exciting runner of his generation from the full-back position. Some could charge into the three-quarter line to make overlaps; others could make courageous high catches; but his great quality was to start unlikely counterattacks from deep in defence, often from standing starts, and with pace and guile spark off spectacular scores at the other end of the pitch.

JEFFREY 1986-90

- Born Kelso 15 March 1959

- Kelso, Scotland and British Lions

- 40 Caps, 11 tries for Scotland

- British Lions tour to Australia 1989, British Lions test vs. Rest of World XV 1986

JOHN JEFFREY holds the Scottish record for most-capped flanker for good reason. His immense stamina and ability to close down and counter his opponent's attacking chances were one of the best features of his game. As well as this, he had the ability to score, points, holding the record for highest scoring Scotland flanker along with Derek White. In his eight years with the Scottish side, John Jeffrey made vast contributions to every tournament that he was involved with, such as the classic Calcutta Cup match in 1990, proving his unfailing commitment to the sport.

LAIDLAW 1980-88

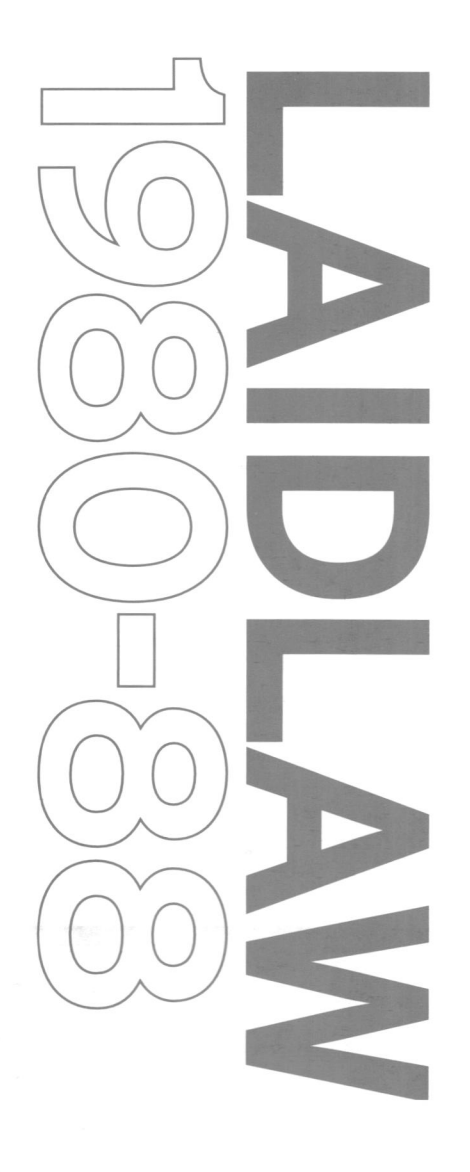

- Born Jedburgh, October 10th 1953

- Jed-Forest, South of Scotland, Scotland and British Lions

- Scrum half in 47 International matches, scored 7 tries

- British Lions New Zealand 1983, 4 tests

ROY LAIDLAW was one of the Scotland side's most powerful attacking assets as his threat to any opposing side as scrum half, and his incredibly successful partnership with John Rutherford, meant that he was involved in some great victories, including the Grand Slam of 1984, during which he scored two tries in the 32-9 victory over Ireland. His breaks from the scrum at high speed, and his consistent team play mark him out as one of the finest ever Scottish players at scrum half.

MAIR 1951

- Born Edinburgh October 7th 1928

- Edinburgh University, Melrose, South of Scotland, Scotland

- 4 International caps as hooker for Scotland, 1951

NORMAN MAIR the writer and broadcaster, played rugby and cricket for Scotland. He was a hard-working and skilled player at hooker, and played in four international Tests for his country.

In 1998, he was appointed to the five-strong Lord Mackay panel which was set up to make a comprehensive review of the state and structure of Scottish rugby.

For some 30 years, he was the rugby and golf correspondent of The Scotsman. Among assorted awards, he was Scotland's Sports Journalist of the year for four years in succession.

McGEECHAN 1974-90

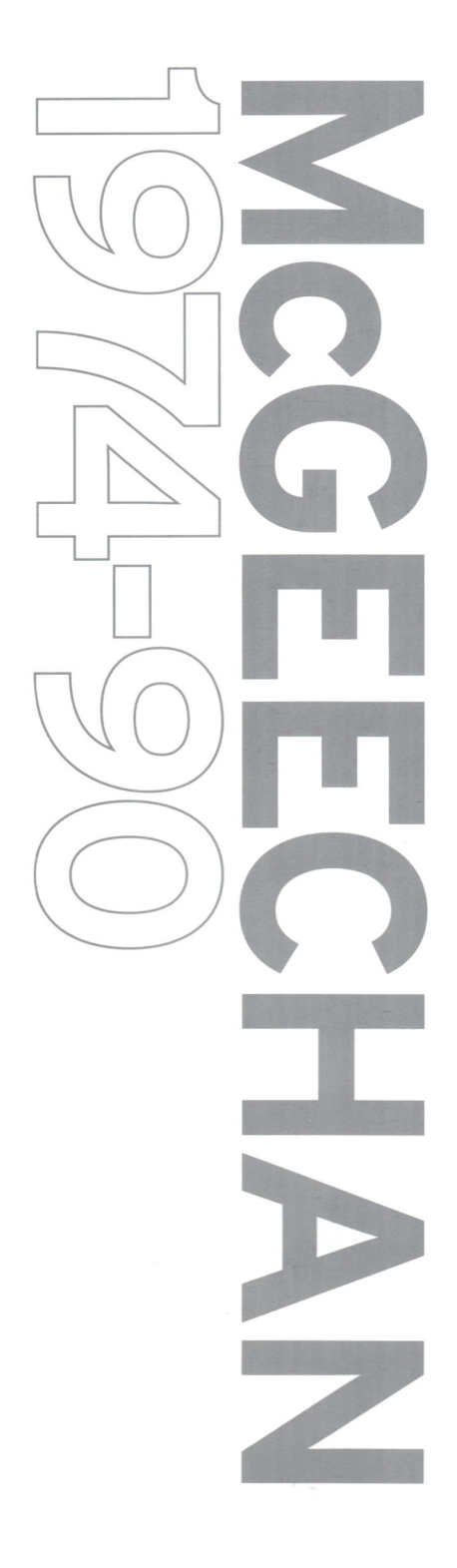

- Born Leeds 30th October 1946

- Headingley, Yorkshire, Scotland and British Lions

- 32 Scottish caps – 20 at centre, 12 at stand-off, with 9 of these as captain

- British Lions 1970 New Zealand, 1974 South Africa

IAN MCGEECHAN played at stand-off and centre, and was an elusive runner on the attack and a superb tackler in defence. As an excellent left-footed kicker he scored seven drop goals in his test career. He now coaches the Scotland national side, and was at the helm for Scotland's Grand Slam victory in 1990. He has become one of the most influential rugby coaches in the world, and coached a record three British Lions tours, to Australia in 1989, New Zealand in 1993 and South Africa in 1997.

McLAUCHLAN 1969-79

- Born Tarbolton, Ayrshire 14th April 1942

- Jordanhill, Glasgow, Scotland and British Lions

- Prop, 43 International caps, 19 as captain

- British Lions tours to New Zealand 1971 and South Africa 1974

IAN MCLAUCHLAN became known as the 'Mighty Mouse' due to his strength and skill in the scrum. With his fiery dedication to the sport, it is perhaps little wonder that he captained Scotland in nearly half of the 43 Internationals that he played in. He is regarded as one of the best props of all time, and participated in some great successes, notably forming part of the only British Lions team ever to come home unbeaten from the tour of South Africa in 1974.

RUTHERFORD
1979-87

- Born Selkirk October 10th 1955

- Selkirk, South of Scotland, Scotland and British Lions

- Stand-off, 42 International caps, 7 tries, 12 drop goals

- British Lions 1983 New Zealand

JOHN RUTHERFORD won 42 caps at the stand-off position, which was a record at the time, and also a demonstration of what a crucial role he played in that position throughout his International career (1979-1987). He developed into one of the finest drop-goal scorers in history, but was equally competent running on or off the ball, to ensure that the opposing defence was thwarted. His reading of any game situation, and his long-running playing partnership with Roy Laidlaw at scrum half ensure that he is considered to be one of the greats.

TELFER 1964-70

- Born Pathhead, Midlothian 17th March 1940

- Melrose, South of Scotland, Scotland and British Lions

- No. 8 and Flanker, 25 Scotland caps, 3 tries (9 points)

- British Lions tours to Australia and New Zealand 1964, and South Africa 1968

JIM TELFER Scotland forwards coach and SRU Director of Rugby, is amongst the top forwards coaches in the world. He was a tirelessly mobile No. 8 and blindside flanker who had an unfailing willingness to put his body on the line for the game. The former Scottish captain was a bloodcurdling motivator, and believed devoutly in good body positions and in rucking with a real hit in it. His numerous coaching credits include the 1983 British Lions tour to New Zealand, and the victorious 1997 tour to South Africa as forwards coach.

ALAN SHAW ROUNDS UP LAST YEAR'S HECTIC SCOTTISH INTERNATIONAL SEASON

In a busier than average international season Scotland played 12 Tests, including the now-annual summer challenge match against the Barbarians, and fielded no fewer than four different captains.

Scotland's season shows a record of five wins and five losses under the successive stewardships of Budge Pountney, Tom Smith, Bryan Redpath and Stuart Grimes. This record, allied to a points tally that read 300 for, with 262 against, tells the story of a year that did not begin as we would have wished but ended well, with much to be positive about as we build towards next summer's World Cup.

We saw many Dark Blue debutants; and some of these players will build on the experience gained on the North American tour to challenge for a seat on the plane to Australia. Also, in a combative pack Scott Murray battled back from his Lions disappointment to win The Famous Grouse Player of the Year Award for an unprecedented second time. Gregor Townsend, meanwhile, became the most-capped Scot in history when he made his 66th appearance with the match against Wales.

SIX NATIONS

SCOTLAND 3 ENGLAND 29
Murrayfield, Saturday, February 2, 2002

Princess Anne shaking hands with Brendan Laney

UNDOUBTEDLY THE most disappointing performance of the season, Scotland handed the Auld Enemy victory on a plate with a display that left much room for improvement.

Duncan Hodge landed only one penalty. Fortunately England had their own handling problems but Clive Woodward's squad looked lively in the open spaces out wide as Jason 'Billy Whizz' Robinson caught the eye with a sparkling brace.

Gregor Townsend on the charge

Chris Paterson shows Austin Healey a clean pair of heels

SCOTLAND 29 ITALY 12
Stadio Flaminio, Saturday, February 16, 2002

George Graham probing the Italian defence

BRENDAN LANEY notched 24 points through a try he described as "lucky", two conversions and five penalties – a Scotland Six Nations record – and was slapped in the chops by an Italian fan on the final whistle for his trouble! Perhaps the Azzurri supporter was irate that Scotland should choose Rome to enjoy their first away win for three years with Scotland's other points coming courtesy of Gregor Townsend's 16th Test touchdown.

Brendan Laney goes over for a try

Glenn Metcalfe clears an Italian defender

Gregor Townsend clears

SIX NATIONS
IRELAND 43 SCOTLAND 22
Lansdowne Road, Saturday, March 2, 2002

THE Jekyll and Hyde season continued in Dublin, where Scotland again gave the win away with a lacklustre performance. Mind you, Ireland needed little help as Leinster wunderkind Brian O'Driscoll ran in a hat trick and created mayhem in the Scots' ranks whenever he was on the ball. Budge Pountney was sinbinned as the visitors' frustrations grew and, with Martin Leslie claiming a single late try, only Brendan Laney's 17-point kicking haul gave any gloss to the scoreline.

Andrew Henderson challenged by David Humphreys

Bryan Redpath on the attack

SIX NATIONS

SCOTLAND 10 FRANCE 22
Murrayfield, Saturday, March 23, 2002

ANOTHER LOSS, but this was a far better game and a much-improved display than the scoreboard would suggest. France were firing on all cylinders but their talented team was made to work hard for the win as Scotland rued some costly handling errors.

Many of the home side impressed but pick of the bunch was skipper Bryan Redpath who had his best international game for some time and scored his first Test try at the 44th time of asking.

Glenn Metcalfe making in roads into the French defence

Budge Pountney gets wrapped up by the French defence

Jason White looking for space

SIX NATIONS
WALES 22 SCOTLAND 27
Millennium Stadium, Saturday, April 6, 2002

Brendan Laney aiming to increase his score count

FITTINGLY, in the land where the fly half is king Gregor Townsend overtook Scott Hasting's 65-cap mark and the Scots celebrated in style with a dramatic win – the first time we'd recorded two away wins since 1990.

Gordon Bulloch was twice driven over for tries and Duncan Hodge's first act after coming on for the injured Laney was to slot the decisive injury-time kick. As it turned out, this was to be John Leslie's 23rd and last cap as he retired after four seasons in the Scotland squad.

Scott Murray claims the ball for Scotland

Bryan Redpath passes the ball to his backs as they attack the Welsh line

BARBARIANS 47 SCOTLAND 27
Murrayfield, Saturday, June 1, 2002

Mike Blair at pace

Nathan Hines

MEN AGAINST boys at Murrayfield with eight uncapped Scots stripped to face their vastly experienced opponents. So, as well as providing quality entertainment, this fixture afforded us a glimpse into the not-so-distant future. New kids on the block Rory Kerr, Andy Craig and Mike Blair – who scored a try – all put down impressive markers and Blair would go on to feature as the first-choice scrum half on the summer tour. Chris 'Mossy' Paterson touched down too, as did Brendan Laney who looked more comfortable switched from full back to inside centre.

Craig Smith is tackled by Percy Montgomery

Chris Paterson struggles to escape the Canadian defence

SUMMER TOUR
CANADA 26 SCOTLAND 23
Thunderbird Stadium, Saturday June 15, 2002

Mike Blair in the Canadian's grasp

SCOTLAND SUFFERED one of their most humiliating defeats despite Stuart Grimes' side outscoring the unfancied Canucks three tries to two in Vancouver. Five-pointers from Chris Paterson, Mike Blair and Simon Taylor seemed to have the Scots in the driving seat at 23-13 to the good, but the tourists lost their shape – and their unbeaten record since arriving in North America – as the second half wore on.

Allan Jacobsen uses his strength to break the Canadian defence

SUMMER TOUR
USA 23 SCOTLAND 65
Balboa Stadium, Saturday June 22, 2002

Allan Jacobsen on the charge

Nathan Hines scores

Andy Craig breaking a tackle

THIS WAS much more like it, although Nathan Hines became the first ever Scotsman sent off in an International for laying out his provoker with a better punch than anything mustered by Audley Harrison. This couldn't take the shine off, however, as Scotland were actually better following his dismissal just before half time! A young and experimental XV came together in San Francisco to record a 10-try win as Duncan Hodge and Chris Paterson (two apiece) plus Brendan Laney, Rory Kerr, Nathan Hines, Andy Henderson, Andy Craig and Jason White went over.

SCOTLAND 37 ROMANIA 10
Murrayfield, Sunday, November 10, 2002

Bryan Redpath

Nikki Walker on the run

Ben Hinshelwood breaking away from the Romanian's grasp

A SLIGHTLY disappointing result for Scotland, despite the scoreline, as this match saw the Scot's preparations for the South Africa game upset by a few problems with rhythm and ball control. Scotland also had injury problems as prop Mattie Stewart sustained a rib injury that might put him out of action for several months. Despite this, there were excellent test debuts for winger Nikki Walker, prop Bruce Douglas and Stuart Moffat who closed the game with an excellent try.

SCOTLAND 21 SOUTH AFRICA 6
Murrayfield Saturday 16th November 2002

Bryan Redpath and his team mates celebrate their victory

Gordon Bulloch

A SUPERB victory for the Scots, and their first win against the South Africans for 33 years, as the Southern Hemisphere giants came to Edinburgh, and discovered the 'Fortress Murrayfield' of old. The Scotland forwards kept the South African pack firmly on the defensive, and Brendan Laney maintained the pressure with a remarkable kicking display, notching up three penalties and a conversion. Budge Pountney opened the try scoring in the second half, with Nikki Walker going over late in the game, and hooker Gordon Bulloch gaining a much-deserved man of the match award.

Simon Taylor on the charge

Gordon Bullock celebrates

SCOTLAND 36 FIJI 22
Murrayfield, Sunday 24th November 2002

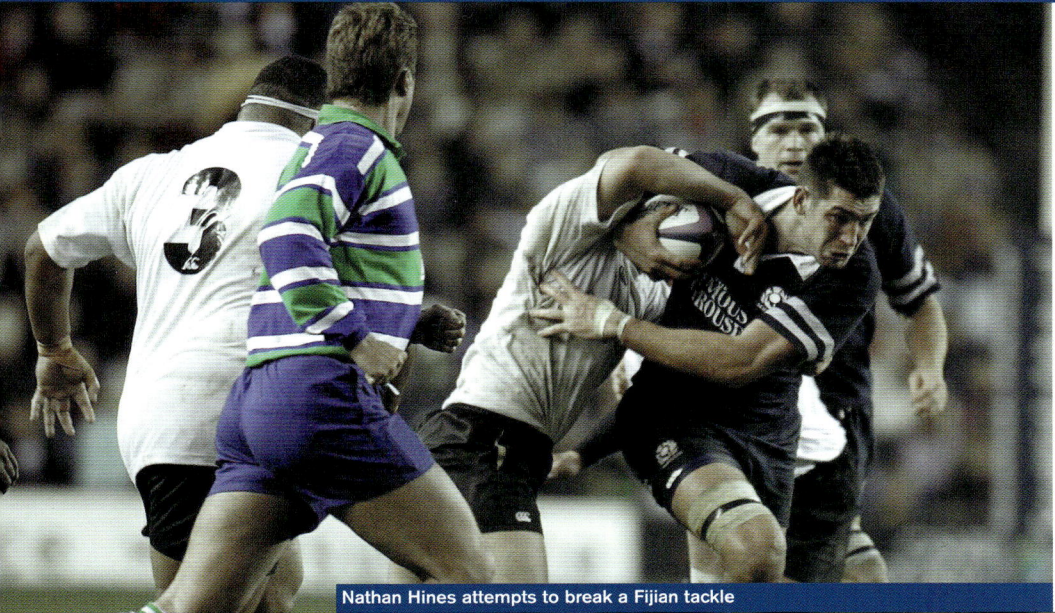

SCOTLAND COMPLETED a record triple win in the Scottish Mutual Autumn Tests with this victory over the Fijians, but the match saw Fiji improving with every second after their defeats by Wales and Ireland. The Scots suffered slightly after some handling mistakes and the Fijians pounced on every chance to make this victory as tough as possible for the home side. However, tries from Brendan Laney, Stuart Gimes and three from Andy Craig ensured a memorable autumn series ended with three wins from three matches.

Nathan Hines attempts to break a Fijian tackle

Andy Craig puts five more points on the board

Tom Smith gets through the Fijian defence

04 THE COMMONWEALTH SEVENS

ALAN SHAW SUMS UP A MIXED COMMONWEALTH GAMES APPEARANCE BY THE SCOTTISH RUGBY SEVENS SIDE.

Marcus Di Rollo, top points-scorer at the Commonwealth Games Rugby Sevens, summed up Scotland's campaign best when he said, "We are a better team than finishing ninth."

Di Rollo's 66-point haul, comprising 6 tries and 18 conversions, was another milestone for the Edinburgh centre after winning his first full cap against the USA just over a month previously, while the Scots' impressive 40-26 victory over Tonga in the Final of the consolation Bowl went some way to making up for the summer's second dose of Canadian woe.

For, coming hot on the heels of the senior XV's shock defeat in Vancouver during the North American tour, it was a disappointing 7-0 loss to the Canucks in Scotland's second Pool A game that saw them fail to qualify for the quarter-finals of the main Medal competition.

That apart, Sevens manager Roy Laidlaw could be pleased with his squad's efforts. In a difficult pool, they kicked off with an eight-try, 54-5 win over South Sea islanders Niue before bowing out into the Bowl tourney with a creditable 26-12 loss to eventual gold-medallists New Zealand.

On their way to bagging the Bowl, Scotland disposed of Sri Lanka - running up 57 points without reply - and enjoyed a 26-7 semi-final win against the Cook Islands.

In the Final itself, Sean Lamont's try brace stole the plaudits and his performances over the three days helped land the young full-back a pro contract with Rotherham.

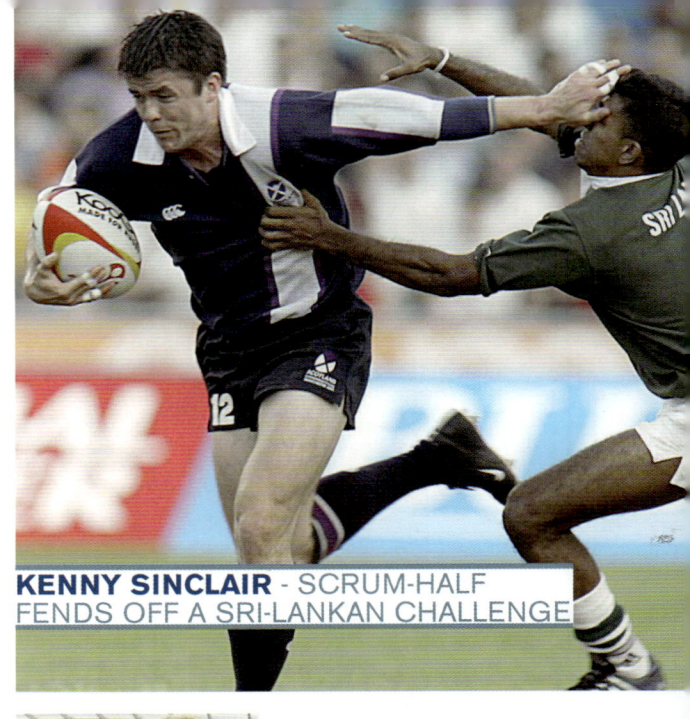

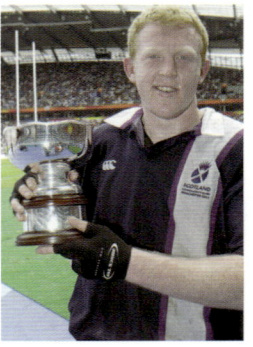

KENNY SINCLAIR - SCRUM-HALF FENDS OFF A SRI-LANKAN CHALLENGE

MARK LEE - SCOTLAND SEVENS CAPTAIN WITH THE COMMONWEALTH GAMES BOWL TROPHY

MARCUS DI ROLLO - ON THE ATTACK AGAINST TONGA

By **ALAN SHAW** rugby writer for *The Sunday Post*

SIMON TAYLOR - BROUGHT INTERNATIONAL EXPERIENCE FROM THE XV-A-SIDE ARENA TO SCOTLAND'S SEVENS SQUAD

THE NEW PEUGEOT 807.
THINK ABOUT IT. WE HAVE.

www.peugeot.co.uk

GUARDIAN ANGELS? This is the first MPV in Europe to feature curtain airbags that cover all three rows of seats.
TELEKINETIC POWERS? For rear doors that mysteriously slide open automatically, press the plip key.**
SIXTH SENSE? Nope. An extra child-check mirror. Common sense.**
MIRACLES? Optional roof-mounted video screen to keep the kids quiet. (Hallelujah.)**
MONEY = HAPPINESS? It does when you have 0% finance over 4 years.*

807

THE DRIVE OF YOUR LIFE.

PEUGEOT

Peugeot 807 Range from £18,295 MRRP on the road, (Peugeot 807 LX 2.0 litre petrol). (Model shown Peugeot 807 Exec 2.2 HDi at £23,555 MRRP on the road, with triple sunroofs 1 front and 2 rear electric tilt and slide at an additional extra cost of £990 MRRP on the road and metallic paint at an additional cost of £275 MRRP.) Prices correct at time of going to press. For more information call 0845 200 1234 or visit www.peugeot.co.uk Official Fuel Economy Figures in mpg (litres/100km) for Peugeot 807 range are: Urban 20.62 – 30.05 (13.7 – 9.4); Extra Urban 36.21 – 47.88 (7.8 – 5.9); Combined 29.12 – 39.23 (9.7 – 7.2) and CO₂ emissions are 189 – 231 (g/km). Optional roof-mounted video screen and DVD player available at £2,199 MRRP on the GLX, Exec and Exec SE excluding those fitted with triple sunroofs. *Finance subject to status. Written quotations available on request from Peugeot Financial Services, Quadrant House, Princess Way, Redhill RH1 1QA. A guarantee may be required. Over 18s only. Retail customers only. 0% finance example for this vehicle is as follows: Vehicle price £23,555 on the road, minimum deposit 35% (£8,244.25), 48 monthly repayments of £318.97, total amount repayable £23,555. **APR 0%.** On the road price is based on Manufacturer's Recommended Retail Price (MRRP) and includes delivery to dealership, number plates, 12 months' Government Vehicle Excise Duty and £25.00 Government First Registration Fee and applies to 807 Exec 2.2 HDi at £23,555 MRRP. Offer available on models ordered and registered between 1st January 2003 and 31st March 2003 inclusive. **Features and options described may not be available on all models in the 807 range. Please consult your local Peugeot dealer for full information on model specifications.

05 SCOTLAND HOME OF SEVENS

A BRIEF HISTORY OF SEVENS

In 1883, in the small town of Melrose in the Borders a new version of the sport we know and love was created – the rugby sevens tournament.

The Melrose club had severe financial problems in that year, until Ned Haig and David Sanderson, both star players in the Melrose full side, came up with the idea of a club sports tournament, running for one day and featuring many of the surrounding Borders teams. The Melrose committee applauded their plan, but expressed their reservations about the practicality of playing a whole full-side tournament in one day.

After discussion by the Committee, a special set of rules was suggested for the one-day event, to enable all of the teams to participate in the time available. There were to be fewer penalties, the playing period was to be reduced to 15 minutes, and the players to just seven men. The event itself was a huge success, attracting as many as 2,000 spectators and clubs from all over the Borders including teams from Melrose, Gala, Selkirk, St. Cuthbert's, Earlston and Gala Forest. The inaugural Melrose Sevens cup was presented to the club for the occasion by the Ladies of Melrose, who gave the sports day their fullest support. The cup was finally won by the home team, who played a close match against Gala in the final, with the home Melrose side winning the match in a hotly contested period of play. From an idea that was born as a response to a lack of time and money, the rugby sevens tournament has come a long way since 1883, and is now a firm fixture in any rugby fan's calendar.

The first ever International Sevens tournament was held at Murrayfield in 1973 to celebrate the centenary of the Scottish Rugby Union. Murrayfield also hosted the first Rugby World Cup Sevens tournament in 1993.

THE MELROSE SEVENS TEAM, WINNERS OF THE FIRST EVER MELROSE TOURNAMENT AFTER A CLOSE FINAL WITH THE GALA SIDE

NED HAIG AND **DAVID SANDERSON**, STARS OF THE WINNING HOME TEAM IN THE FIRST EVER COMPETITION FOR THE MELROSE LADIES' CUP

41

06 SIX NATIONS PREVIEW

ALAN LORIMER LOOKS FORWARD TO SCOTLAND'S 2003 RBS SIX NATIONS CAMPAIGN

It's strange how fortunes can change so quickly. Going into the 2002 Six Nations Championship, Scotland had little to lift their spirits after losing to Argentina and New Zealand, and had to draw what comfort they could from the victory over Tonga.

Fast-forward twelve months and suddenly all is different. Scotland's November win over South Africa by 21-6 brought the passion back to Murrayfield and above all offered hope that the dark blues might mount a challenge in the 2003 RBS Six Nations championship. Victory over the Springboks also rolled back history to 1969 when Scotland had last beaten South Africa. At last, Scotland had taken a major southern hemisphere scalp in the professional era.

Scotland's director of rugby, Jim Telfer, had been brought back into the Scots' coaching team to assist Ian McGeechan, and in the event his influence was evident throughout the match as the Scotland forwards proceeded to destroy the Springboks in every phase of play, the two tries - by Budge Pountney and Nikki Walker - both coming from frontal pressure.

The Scots will now go into the RBS Six Nations with a very experienced pack and what is more with experienced benchmen in Jon Petrie, Nathan Hines and David Hilton, the latter resuming his international career after a three year absence, during which he acquired residency qualifications for Scotland.

Telfer and McGeechan formed a formidable coaching duo in South Africa on the 1997 Lions tour. This season it seems the old magic is working again. Sadly the conditions of constant drizzle at Murrayfield for the South Africa Test virtually ruled out constructive back play, leaving a question mark over the Scots' ability to slice through defences.

But what did emerge was the soundness of play at stand-off from Gordon Ross, who was given a second consecutive run in the number 10 position to prove himself at the highest level. In the event Ross controlled matters with an authority that belied his three-cap status and in doing so gave McGeechan genuine options in the stand-off position, for which Gregor Townsend remains in contention for the RBS Six Nations campaign.

The victory over South Africa closely followed Scotland's 37-10 win against Romania and preceded the victory against Fiji completing the Scottish Mutual Autumn Tests at Murrayfield. The scoreline did not match that which Wales had achieved against the Romanians but that mattered little to the Scotland management. What did was trying out a number of new players in a Test match environment.

Victory was also significant psychologically, ending as it did what had been a barren twelve months at Murrayfield without a win. The 5 try victory also allowed McGeechan to achieve continuity in selection ahead of the Springbok Test giving ringing endorsements to new caps Bruce Douglas at tight head, right wing Nikki Walker and full back Stuart Moffat.

Whether this can be translated into success in the 2003 RBS Six Nations Championship remains to be seen. Hopes will be high but the memory of the 2002 championship will still linger on as a reminder that matters must be improved. For 2002 was a championship that had promised much for Scotland but which in the end produced a 4th finishing place for the Scots, an outcome that fell hugely below the hopes of both the coaching team and the large army of tartan fans.

Worse for the home supporters was the absence of a Murrayfield victory as Scotland succumbed all too easily to England in the opening round in Edinburgh and then to France in a forgettable game two rounds later.

IAN MCGEECHAN - THE SOONER WE GET TO FOUR PROFESSIONAL SIDES IN SCOTLAND, THE BETTER. I BELIEVE THAT THE COMMITMENT TO CREATING A FOURTH TEAM IS NOW THERE

SCOTLAND'S NOVEMBER WIN OVER SOUTH AFRICA BY 21-6 BROUGHT THE PASSION BACK TO MURRAYFIELD AND ABOVE ALL OFFERED HOPE THAT THE DARK BLUES MIGHT MOUNT A CHALLENGE IN THE 2003 RBS SIX NATIONS CHAMPIONSHIP

SCOTLAND'S VICTORY OVER FIJI COMPLETED A SUCCESSFUL AUTUMN CAMPAIGN LAYING THE FOUNDATIONS FOR SUCCESS IN 2003

CALVIN HOWARTH HAS BEEN ADDED TO THE SCOTLAND SQUAD THIS SEASON

All that Scotland's faithful were left to savour was a 29-12 win in Italy courtesy of an interception try by Gregor Townsend at a stage when the match was finely balanced plus a late score by Brendan Laney, and a 27-22 victory in Cardiff.

Sandwiched in between these two successes was a dismal display in Dublin that resulted in a heavy 43-22 win for Ireland and further evidence that Scottish back play was slipping woefully behind world standards.

So can Scotland press the delete button on a disappointing 2002 campaign and look for better results this season? Certainly home advantage, which failed to work in favour of Scotland last year, should do so this season. Scotland face Ireland, Wales and Italy in Edinburgh where their record against all three nations is good.

The greater problems for Scotland are likely to be at Twickenham against England and at the Stade de France against the defending champions. Twickenham, especially, is a formidable fortress, and a constant psychological barrier for the Scots.

Time alone does not improve matters for Scotland. What does, however, is the fast tracking of emergent talent and increasing the pool of potential international players. To these ends Scotland coach Ian McGeechan is in a healthier position this season than twelve months ago.

What has made selection better for McGeechan this season is the extra competition for places that has been created by the setting up of Scotland's third professional side, The Borders. Hitherto Scotland qualified players from the two pro sides - Edinburgh and Glasgow - were virtually guaranteed at least an A cap. Now that has changed with the establishment of The Borders.

"Having a third home-based professional side this season means that there is greater competition for places. In many ways the third team opens the door for opportunities. The sooner we get to four professional sides in Scotland, the better. I believe that the commitment to creating a fourth team is now there," suggested the Scotland coach.

Greater competition for international places will be just one of the factors that points to a better performing Scotland team.

What McGeechan is seeking is a fundamental improvement in performance that will be reflected in genuinely convincing results. To that end the Scotland coach is seeking a higher level of fitness in his squad.

There were times when you could see frustration pouring out of McGeechan as his players failed to carry out his game plan; one, as he outlined recently, which is based on speed.

He said: "I like quick teams. Not necessarily quick players but sides that overall are fast. Sometimes last season there were signs that we were not fit enough and that led to mistakes. I want to raise the level of fitness in the squad. I believe we've already improved it significantly.

"Fitness must relate to what we're trying to do. It's about the length of time you can continue a move and about the intensity you put into the game," added the Scotland coach.

A memory of Dublin last season will doubtlessly exemplify what McGeechan is getting at. Then Scotland's lack of sharpness, leading to an error-filled performance, and an obvious lack of pace in midfield were cruelly exposed.

So much of the midfield magic is, of course, down to the choice of stand-off and in this respect McGeechan has widened his options with the introduction of Gordon Ross of Leeds Tykes (and to the enlarged squad the introduction of Calvin Howarth, the Glasgow no. 10) to exert pressure on Gregor Townsend.

ANOTHER RISING STAR MAKING AN IMPRESSION IS WINGER **NIKKI WALKER**, WHO WAS ON THE SCOTLAND TOUR TO NORTH AMERICA IN JUNE AND SCORED AGAINST THE SPRINGBOKS IN NOVEMBER

Come racing in Scotland

SCOTTISH RACING

AYR • HAMILTON PARK • KELSO • MUSSELBURGH • PERTH

www.scottishracing.co.uk

FIXTURE LIST

Thu 2 Jan	Ayr	Jump
Fri 10 Jan	Kelso	Jump
Fri 17 Jan	Musselburgh	Jump
Sat 25 Jan	Ayr	Jump
Tue 28 Jan	Musselburgh	Jump
Thu 30 Jan	Kelso	Jump
Mon 3 Feb	Musselburgh	Jump
Sat 8 Feb	Ayr	Jump
Wed 12 Feb	Musselburgh	Jump
Sat 22 Feb	Musselburgh	Jump
Sat 1 Mar	Kelso	Jump
Fri 7 Mar	Ayr	Jump
Sat 8 Mar	Ayr	Jump
Fri 21 Mar	Kelso	Jump
Thu 27 Mar	Musselburgh	Flat
Mon 7 Apr	Kelso	Jump
Thu 10 Apr	Musselburgh	Flat
Fri 11 Apr	Ayr	Jump
Sat 12 Apr	Ayr	Jump
Wed 23 Apr	Perth	Jump
Thur 24 Apr	Perth	Jump
Fri 25 Apr	Perth	Jump
Mon 28 Apr	Hamilton Park	Flat
Wed 23 Apr	Perth	Jump
Wed 30 Apr	Kelso	Jump (Eve)
Fri 2 May	Musselburgh	Flat
Sun 4 May	Hamilton Park	Flat
Wed 7 May	Kelso	Jump
Fri 9 May	Hamilton Park	Flat (Eve)
Wed 14 May	Perth	Jump (Eve)
Thu 15 May	Perth	Jump
Fri 16 May	Hamilton Park	Flat (Eve)
Sat 17 May	Hamilton Park	Flat
Mon 19 May	Musselburgh	Flat (Eve)
Wed 21 May	Kelso	Jump
Thu 22 May	Kelso	Jump (Eve)
Thu 29 May	Ayr	Flat
Fri 30 May	Ayr	Flat
Sat 31 May	Musselburgh	Flat
Thu 5 Jun	Perth	Jump
Fri 6 Jun	Perth	Jump (Eve)
Wed 11 Jun	Hamilton Park	Flat (Eve)
Thu 12 Jun	Hamilton Park	Flat
Mon 16 Jun	Musselburgh	Flat
Wed 18 Jun	Hamilton Park	Flat
Thu 19 Jun	Ayr	Flat (Eve)
Fri 20 Jun	Ayr	Flat
Sat 21 Jun	Ayr	Flat
Sun 22 Jun	Perth	Jump
Mon 23 Jun	Musselburgh	Flat
Thu 26 Jun	Hamilton Park	Flat (Eve)
Mon 30 Jun	Musselburgh	Flat (Eve)
Tue 1 Jul	Hamilton Park	Flat
Wed 2 Jul	Perth	Jump
Thu 3 Jul	Perth	Jump
Mon 7 July	Musselburgh	Flat
Fri 11 Jul	Hamilton Park	Flat (Eve)
Mon 14 Jul	Ayr	Flat
Thu 17 July	Hamilton Park	Flat
Fri 18 July	Hamilton Park	Flat (Eve)
Mon 21 Jul	Ayr	Flat
Tue 22 Jul	Ayr	Flat
Thu 24 Jul	Hamilton Park	Flat (Eve)
Thu 31 Jul	Musselburgh	Flat (Eve)
Fri 1 Aug	Ayr	Flat (Eve)
Wed 13 Aug	Hamilton Park	Flat (Eve)
Sat 16 Aug	Perth	Jump
Tue 19 Aug	Hamilton Park	Flat
Thu 21 Aug	Musselburgh	Flat
Fri 29 Aug	Ayr	Flat
Mon 1 Sep	Hamilton Park	Flat
Sat 13 Sep	Musselburgh	Flat
Wed 24 Sep	Perth	Jump
Thu 25 Sep	Perth	Jump
Mon 15 Sep	Musselburgh	Flat
Thu 18 Sep	Ayr	Flat
Fri 19 Sep	Ayr	Flat
Sat 20 Sep	Ayr	Flat
Sun 28 Sep	Musselburgh	Flat
Mon 29 Sep	Hamilton Park	Flat
Sun 5 Oct	Kelso	Jump
Mon 13 Oct	Ayr	Flat
Tue 14 Oct	Ayr	Flat
Sat 18 Oct	Kelso	Jump
Sat 25 Oct	Musselburgh	Flat
Sat 1 Nov	Kelso	Jump
Wed 5 Nov	Musselburgh	Flat
Wed 12 Nov	Kelso	Jump
Sat 15 Nov	Ayr	Jump
Sun 16 Nov	Ayr	Jump
Fri 28 Nov	Musselburgh	Jump
Mon 1 Dec	Kelso	Jump
Mon 8 Dec	Ayr	Jump
Tue 16 Dec	Musselburgh	Jump
Fri 26 Dec	Ayr	Jump
Tue 30 Dec	Musselburgh	Jump

New Zealand-born Howarth, who qualified for Scotland through residency last August, will add to the healthy competition between the two capped stand-offs, while, as McGeechan has indicated, there remains too the possibility of deploying Duncan Hodge.

In the wider sphere, another newcomer this season is the Hawick centre Stephen Cranston. The son of the former Scotland centre Alastair Cranston, Stephen is a quicker player than his father but just as ferocious a tackler.

Centre was a problem position for Scotland last season and it would seem that it offers the best chance for young players to establish themselves in the senior side. Cranston may have to work his apprenticeship in the A team but he is certainly one of the new brigade worth watching and one who could make the World Cup squad.

Another rising star from the Hawick stable is the 6'4" winger Nikki Walker, who, like Cranston is contracted to The Borders. Walker went on the Scotland tour to North America in June and made a sufficient impression to assure him of a place in the team this season.

Yet another player who has advanced his career this season is Ben Hinshelwood, the Worcester wing/full back, whose father Sandy was a Scotland and British Lions Test player, and who gained caps in the Autumn Tests.

At the beginning of the season it seemed there would be healthy competition at scrum half but such has been the form of Bryan Redpath and the authority of his leadership that the claims of Michael Blair of Edinburgh and Graeme Beveridge of Glasgow may have to be put on hold. But for McGeechan the luxury of having three such good players at his disposal is one for which he could yet be grateful.

Amongst the new challengers in the forwards, Andrew Hall, the Glasgow lock, has been prominent this season after such a fine display by the Scotland pack against South Africa, Hall, who went on tour to North America with Scotland this year, and a lock in the modern idiom - rangy, a skilful handler, and a player with useful pace - may have to join a distinguished queue.

Out of the established group of forwards, McGeechan can call upon Gavin Kerr (Leeds Tykes) and Allan Jacobsen (Edinburgh), and flankers Donnie Macfadyen (Glasgow), Andrew Mower (The Borders) and teenager Allister Hogg (Edinburgh).

A serious challenge in the RBS Six Nations is now overdue and without doubt the fans will be looking for a reinvigorated team capable of making an impact at the World Cup in Australia. Victories were in short supply at Murrayfield last season. The Scottish Mutual Autumn Tests ended the diet of defeat. Now the Scots supporters want not only a continuation of ways, but also a reinfusion of the exhilarating rugby that has been so manifestly missing from the national game. Expectation and demands will indeed be high in the 2003 championship.

AFTER HIS IMPRESSIVE DEBUT IN LAST SEASON'S AUTUMN TESTS **GORDON ROSS** CONTINUES TO CONTRIBUTE GREATLY TO SCOTLAND'S SUCCESS

SCOTLAND'S RBS SIX NATIONS MATCHES

SUNDAY 16 FEBRUARY	vs	IRELAND	AT MURRAYFIELD K.O 15.00
SUNDAY 23 FEBRUARY	vs	FRANCE	AT STADE DE FRANCE K.O 15.00
SATURDAY 8 MARCH	vs	WALES	AT MURRAYFIELD K.O 16.00
SATURDAY 22 MARCH	vs	ENGLAND	AT TWICKENHAM K.O 16.00
SATURDAY 29 MARCH	vs	ITALY	AT MURRAYFIELD K.O 15.00

By **ALAN LORIMER** *The Herald*

07 BARBARIANS PREVIEW

THE SCOTS AND THE BARBARIANS - A HISTORY OF GREAT BATTLES

2002 saw a young Scotland side battling against the experienced Barbarians, and eventually losing 47-27 after a great match

Here's hoping that in May 2003 the record can be set straight by a revitalised Scottish team, following on from their vast successes in November in the Scottish Mutual Autumn Tests. Whilst it's hard to predict the outcome, it will surely depend on how Scotland perform in the RBS Six Nations tournament.

A lot is also riding on the strength of the 2003 Barbarians team, as they have such a wealth of players to select from these days the teams can vary in their competitive strengths. But one thing is certain, the Barbarians' selectors will earmark the players who most enjoy rugby and delight in entertaining; they must, too, possess a high level of individual skill. This ensures that supporters will always get their money's worth, with the likes of Jonah Lomu, Thomas Castaignede, Josh Kronfeld, Lawrence Dallaglio, Simon Taylor and Brian O'Driscoll among the current crop of Baa-Baas stars. The Barbarians' rugby is quite simple about celebrating the game, spreading the keen spirit of a sport which has, for over a century, brought together people of all sizes, backgrounds and nationalities in a common purpose and showing the world just how entertaining rugby can be. The Barbarians don't ignore good forward rugby, but since the club's inception, by founder W. P. Carpmael, in 1890, there has been a willingness to entertain, and it is that concept which creates a mystique around the men who don the black-and-white hooped jerseys.

In fact, it was the Barbarians team which spearheaded the 'eight forwards and seven three-quarters' formation, which became widely accepted and remains still the make-up of Rugby Union teams. The type of flowing attacking rugby that resulted soon became known as 'Barbarian-style' - a phrase used worldwide with 'Barbarian' clubs having sprouted in the leading rugby nations.

JONAH LOMU - A CONSISTENT FEATURE OF THE EXPERIENCED BARBARIANS TEAMS THAT SCOTLAND HAVE FACED

JON PETRIE AND BRENDAN LANEY TACKLE PERCY MONGOMERY OF THE BARBARIANS

On 28 January, 2003, some of the most talented players to have represented the Barbarians meet at the London Hilton for a dinner celebrating the club's most famous victory, the memorable defeat of the 1973 All Blacks which featured THAT length-of-the-field try by Gareth Edwards. Edwards, Willie John McBride, Phil Bennett, JPR Williams, Fergus Slattery, David Duckham and Sandy Carmichael are just some of the most famous names of that magical era.

It further cements the Barbarians' return after an uncertain period since the turbulent advent of professionalism in 1995. With an increasing fixture list of high-profile European Cup and Test matches, there was concern over whether players, coaches and clubs would still release their prized assets for Barbarians' 'friendlies'. We needn't have worried - the Baa-Baas have again been grasped to the bosom as a way of retaining the old values and warm loyalties in an ever-changing environment.

The club, presided over by the popular Micky Steele-Bodger - the first Barbarians player to score, in 1948, against a touring side - has returned to the calendar at the end of the traditional British season and played a major role in raising money for Scottish charities, most recently the Gordon Brown Memorial Endowment Fund.

The sixth clash between Scotland and the Baa-Baas, in 2001, was officially designated by the SRU as the Gordon Brown Memorial International, to honour the Scotland and British Lions forward who died from cancer in March of that year. Scotland coach Ian McGeechan admitted he saw it as fitting that such a player, a former Scotland and Lions teammate, be linked so closely with the Baa-Baas.

He said: "The fact that we're playing the Barbarians, in great sunshine hopefully, is so fitting for this game as it will reflect Gordon's personality. "He always had a smile on his face, and we hope to create rugby that leaves people smiling. I think that would be a great memorial to Gordon Brown."

With Jonah Lomu weighing in with four tries, the Baa-Baas won by the incredible scoreline of 71-34, their all-round skill simply devastating, but few left Murrayfield without smiles that day.

Brown was a keen Barbarians player, but it is legendary wing Arthur Smith, of Cambridge University, who holds the distinction of being Scotland's 'most-capped' Baa-Baa, having played 23 times. Selkirk's Jack Waters played 22 times and Sandy Carmichael 20, whilst Irishman Tony O'Reilly leads the way overall with 30 'caps'.

The Barbarians will tour the UK at the end of May in 2003, playing England at Twickenham on 25 May, Scotland at Murrayfield on 28 May and finishing in the Millennium Stadium with the Welsh on 31 May. Who will play will remain under wraps until close to the tour, but how they will play is no secret. Ready to be excited?

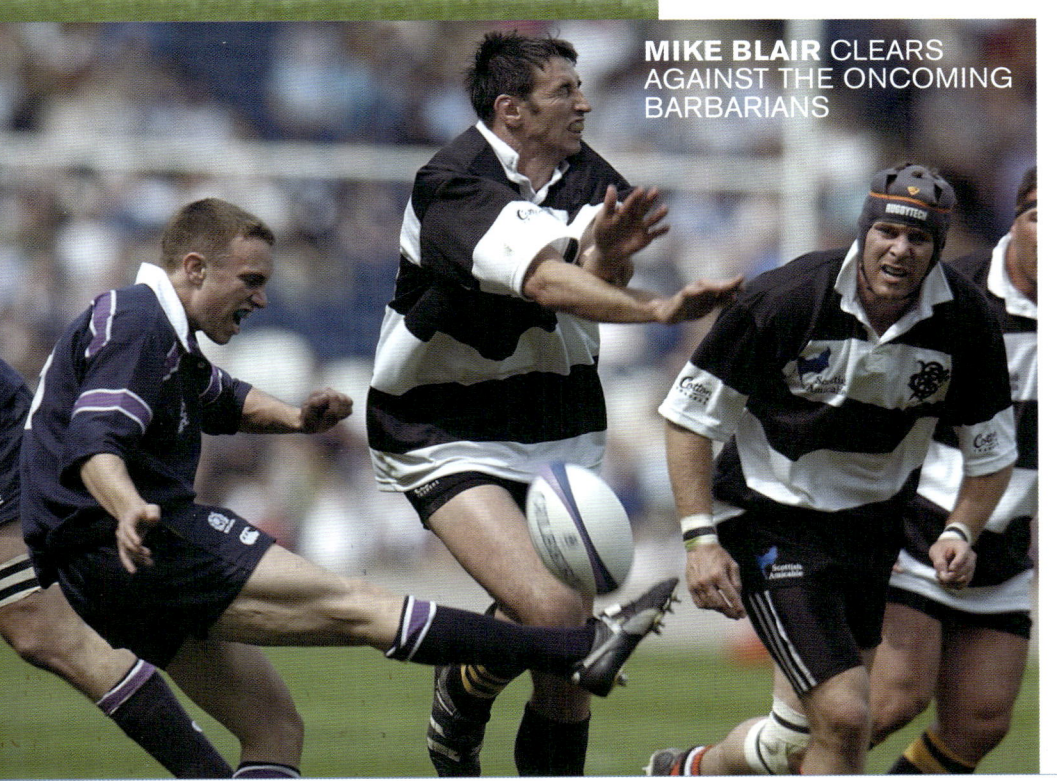

MIKE BLAIR CLEARS AGAINST THE ONCOMING BARBARIANS

By **DAVID FERGUSON** Chief rugby writer for *The Scotsman*

AON

The leading retail insurance broking network in the UK
Specialists in sports risk management

Working in partnership with Scottish Rugby

SCOTTISH RUGBY

Health Select Personal Accident and Income Protection Plans Tel: 0800 169 7700
Professional players personal accident cover Tel: 0131 456 3000
Prestige household insurance Tel: 0131 456 3092

For information on the full range of Aon services available, please visit
www.aon.co.uk
or contact our offices in Edinburgh, Glasgow, Aberdeen and throughout the world

Aon Limited is a member of the General Insurance Standards Council

08 WORLD CUP PREPARATIONS

THE OASIS RESORT - SCOTLAND'S BASE FOR THE FIRST THREE WEEKS OF THE POOLS MATCHES

RETURN TO OZ - IAN MCGEECHAN'S PLANS FOR THE 2003 RUGBY WORLD CUP IN AUSTRALIA

"Tis not in mortals to command success, but we'll do more, Sempronius, we'll deserve it."

The words of Addison came back across the centuries, unbidden, as Ian McGeechan outlined his exhaustive plans for the fifth playing of the World Cup.

It will be his third. He was the assistant coach to Derrick Grant in 1987 when, though the try score was only 0-2, Scotland were beaten 30-3 by New Zealand at Lancaster Park in the quarter-finals of the inaugural tourney. Four years later, he was the senior coach with Jim Telfer as his assistant when Scotland lost 9-6 to England at Murrayfield in an agonisingly close-run, tryless semi-final.

In addition to miscellaneous overseas tours, some as a Scotland or Lions player, he was, uniquely, the Lions' coach on three successive tours. He won five out of nine tests on enemy soil at a time when the players of the Southern Hemisphere were generally held to be markedly superior to their counterparts on the other half of the globe.

He is stepping down as Scotland's coach to become the SRU's Director of Rugby after the World Cup, but in the meantime he is pouring everything he has learned over his own remarkable career into Scotland's preparations.

Remembering how the fact-finding reconnaissance visit he made to South Africa in 1996 paid off in 1997 when the Lions beat all the pre-tour odds to win the Test series at the expense of the reigning World Champions, he travelled to Australia in September 2002. He was accompanied by Scotland's kicking coach, Michael Byrne, an Australian himself with a background mainly in Australian Rules but with useful contacts in his native country's Rugby League and Rugby Union.

McGeechan, of course, was the victorious Lions' coach in Australia, in 1989 while he was back in 1999 for the IRB conference as one of the coaches who made an invaluable contribution to that gathering's adjustment of the contentious latter-day laws regarding the aftermath of a tackle. Nevertheless, as far as the forthcoming World Cup is concerned, he would, but for that September trip down under, have been working blind in all too many respects.

Almost his first move had been to phone two old friends in Rod MacQueen, who had coached the Wallabies to their 1999 World Cup triumph, and the former Australian stand-off, Paul McLean, who had gone on to be a power in Queensland rugby. MacQueen strongly recommended, as Scotland's initial base for the first three weeks of the Pool matches, the Oasis resort at Caloundra.

On the Sunshine Coast, the resort is only an hour North of Brisbane and, as a delighted McGeechan put it, it had everything, including a very good hotel which has its own swimming pool, tennis courts, putting green and a players' room, which will all be at the Scots' disposal.

Just five minutes away is Caloundra Rugby Park with a complex complete with a gymnasium with all the latest equipment in terms of weight training and so forth, a 50 metre swimming pool, another 25 metre swimming pool and a 10 metre by 4 metre rehab pool.

The players will be billeted in the holiday villas, which two can share. Each has its own kitchen facilities. Everybody in this Scottish expeditionary force will have a bike and use it for all local journeys including those to the beach. The only time they will leave their base camp at Caloundra in those opening weeks will be when they fly to Townsville to play Japan at the Dairy Farmers' Stadium.

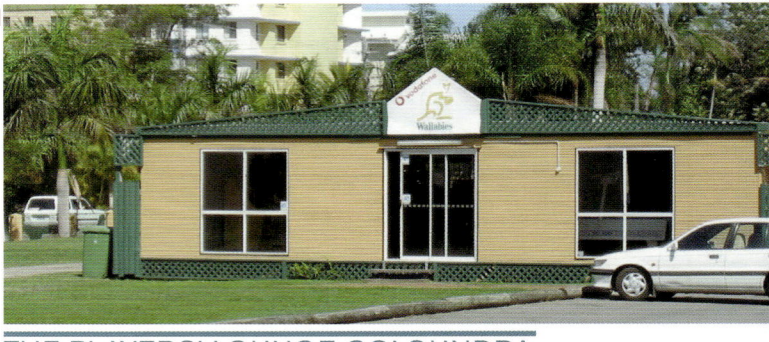

THE PLAYERS' LOUNGE COLOUNDRA

COLOUNDRA TRAINING CENTRE

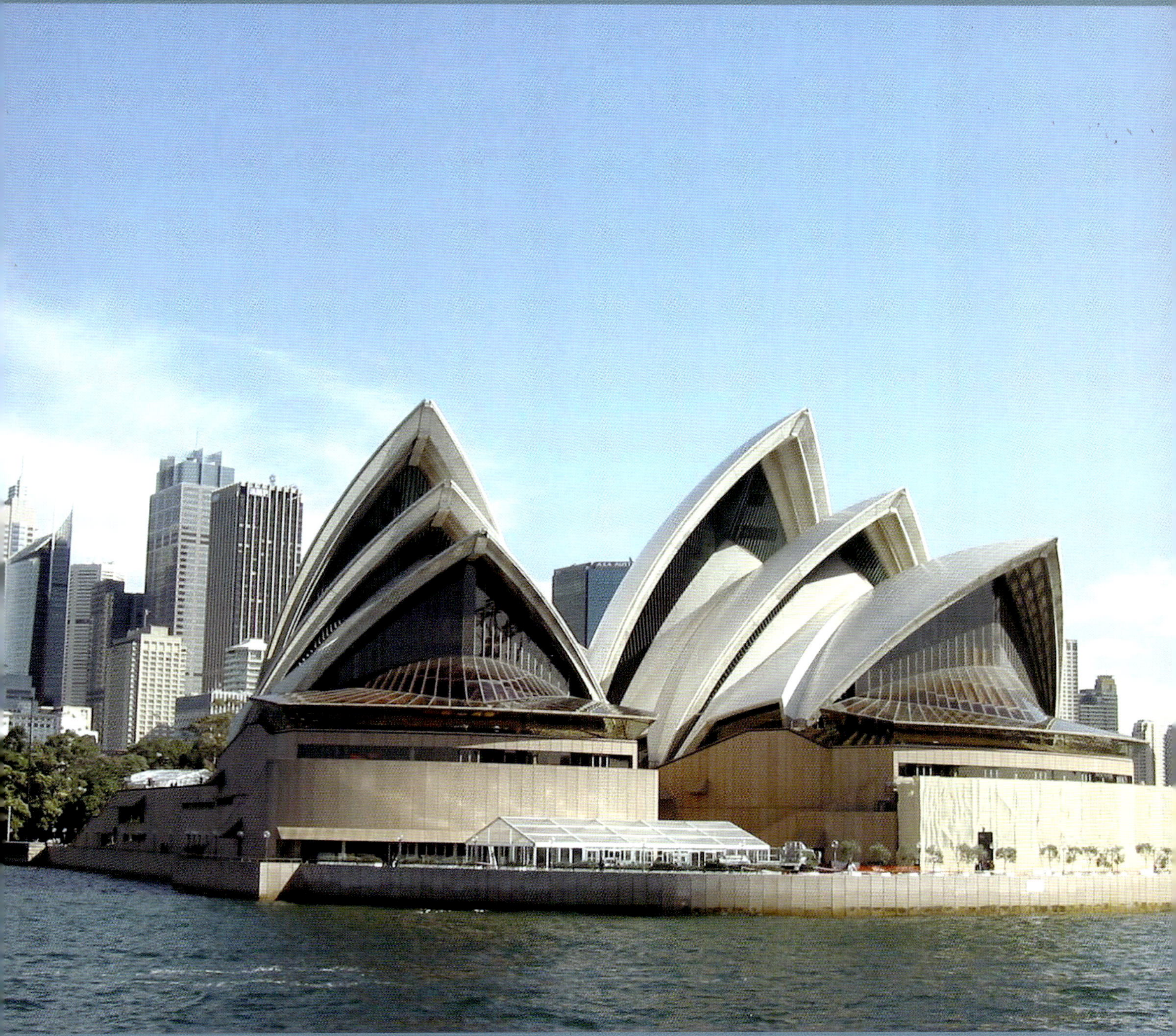

SCOTTISH MUTUAL AUTUMN TESTS WINNERS 2002

THE SCOTLAND RUGBY SUPPORTER'S CLUB

THE PACK

SCOTLAND
RUGBY SUPPORTERS CLUB
sunday mail

THE SQUAD

CALLING ALL SCOTLAND SUPPORTERS!
TO JOIN CALL THE HOTLINE ON
0808 100 1913

SYDNEY FOOTBALL STADIUM

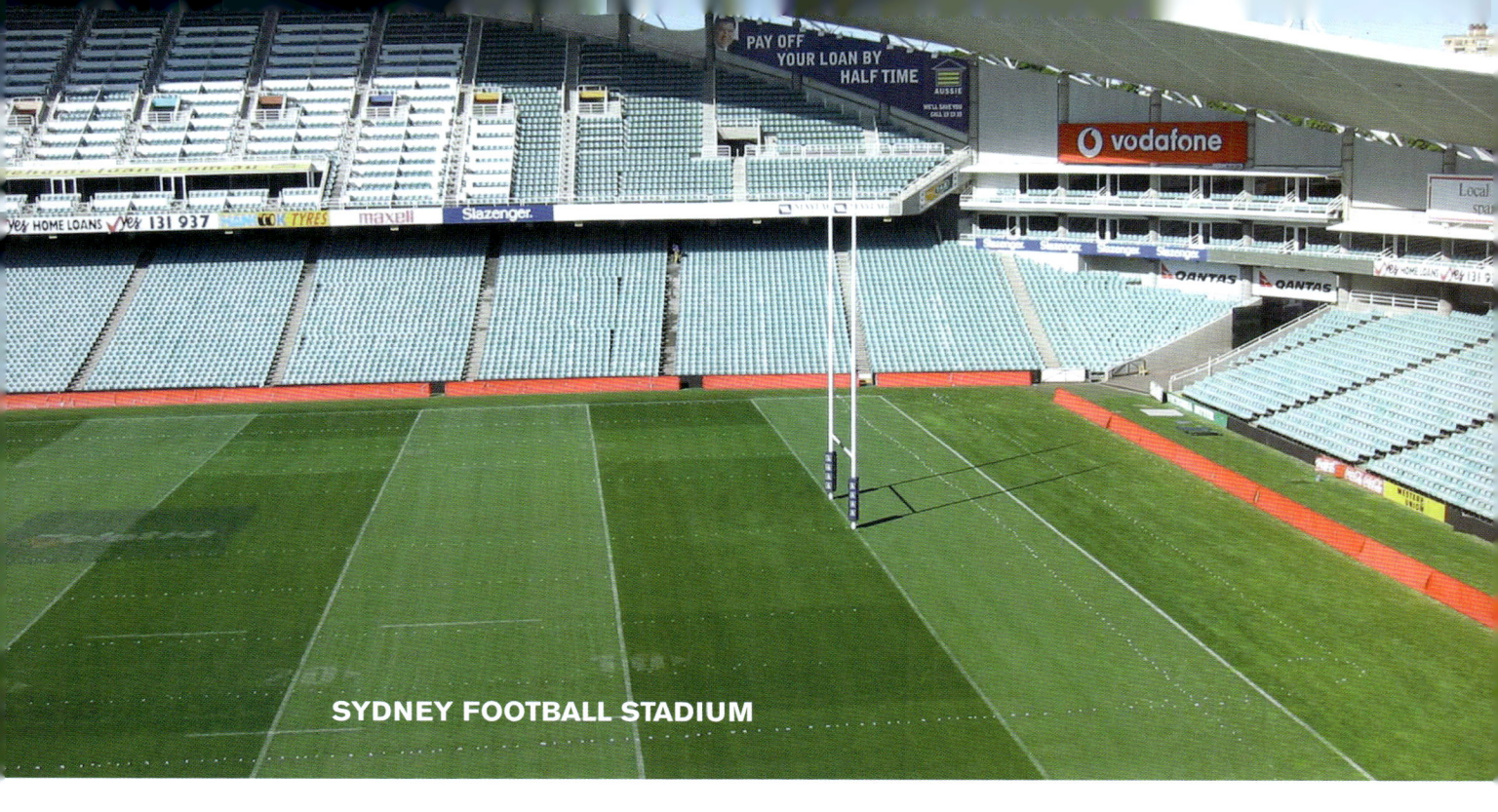

Another helpful contact was the Australian Rugby League coach, Chris Anderson. Taking his advice, the Scots are hoping to stay two weeks at Cronulla for their matches with France and Fiji.

The heat and humidity likely to be encountered in Australia are an issue that the Scotland coaching team is not taking lightly, as McGeechan hopes to have them, in the weeks leading up to their departure for the World Cup, doing some work on cycling and rowing machines in the heat that can be generated in Edinburgh's Botanical gardens. That is how seriously he is taking the problem.

For quite some time, Scotland have been using the new Gilbert ball in practice. It goes farther than it's predecessors but McGeechan's men should be fully accustomed to it by the time they run out against Japan since it is to be the ball employed in the 2003 Royal Bank of Scotland Six Nations.

As for the playing kit, McGeechan has faith in Marty Hulme, the Australian fitness expert who heads the Sale youth academy and who is no stranger to the Scotland squad and Murrayfield. McGeechan and Hulme are still debating the most appropriate fabric to counter the humidity and also the most suitable stockings; one theory being that the hose in question could have something in common with the stockings recommended to offset the danger of deep vein thrombosis on long flights.

With an eye not just to the Royal Bank of Scotland Six Nations but also to the World Cup, Scotland, International commitments permitting, have had fortnightly Monday squad sessions. One admirable feature was that, in the earlier part of the season, a number of youngsters were given the opportunity to train under McGeechan and Telfer alongside seasoned internationals.

The coaches in the accredited 12-strong supporting cast have still not been finalised at the moment of writing, but clearly Pat Lam as well as Jim Telfer will be on the plane.

The extra matches arranged for the months between the end of the Royal Bank of Scotland Six Nations and the Pool matches in the World Cup should prove revealingly testing. One thinks, in particular, of the two games in South Africa, which could be very instructive, given the hard, fast pitches that are likely to greet Scotland there and then in the land of Oz.

THE SIX MATCHES ARE

WEDNESDAY 28 MAY	vs	BARBARIANS	AT MURRAYFIELD
SATURDAY 7 JUNE	vs	SOUTH AFRICA	IN DURBAN
SATURDAY 14 JUNE	vs	SOUTH AFRICA	IN JOHANNESBURG
SATURDAY 23 AUGUST	vs	ITALY	AT MURRAYFIELD
SATURDAY 30 AUGUST	vs	WALES	IN CARDIFF
SATURDAY 6 SEPTEMBER	vs	IRELAND	AT MURRAYFIELD

SCOTLAND'S RWC POOL MATCHES

SUNDAY 12 OCTOBER	vs	JAPAN	AT THE DAIRY FARMERS STADIUM, TOWNSVILLE
MONDAY 20 OCTOBER	vs	REPECHARGE 1	AT SUNCORN MEDWAY STADIUM, BRISBANE
SATURDAY 25 OCTOBER	vs	FRANCE	AT STADIUM AUSTRALIA, SYDNEY
SATURDAY 1 NOVEMBER	vs	FIJI	AT SYDNEY FOOTBALL STADIUM

By **NORMAN MAIR**

09 GLASGOW RUGBY

STUART MOFFAT - A CAMBRIDGE DOUBLE BLUE. HE SCORED JUST A FEW RUNS SHORT OF A DOUBLE CENTURY AGAINST OXFORD AND TWICE FEATURED IN THE OVAL-BALL VERSION OF THE VARSITY MATCH AT TWICKENHAM

DAVID KELSO GIVES HIS VIEW OF GLASGOW'S CONTRIBUTION TO SCOTTISH RUGBY.

They are the Big City Boys - and at last they are living up to that tag. For decades, Glasgow players were regarded as the sleeping giants of Scottish rugby - but not now.

KIWI SEARANCKE HAS RAISED THE PROFILE OF THE GAME IN THE WEST OF THE COUNTRY

The arrival of Kiwi Searancke as head coach of the Warriors pro team has raised the profile of the game in the West of the country and the level of involvement in Ian McGeechan's national squad is on the up and up. The most heartening factor is, perhaps, that so many players are vying for the step up to the Test arena.

Those from Glasgow who have already made the jump include utility back Glenn Metcalfe, wing Jon Steel, centre Alan Bulloch, scrum-half Graeme Beveridge, locks Jason White and Andy Hall, back-rowers Gordon Simpson, Jon Petrie and Donnie Macfadyen - and, of course, old stagers Andy Nicol, Gordon Bulloch and David Hilton.

GRAEME BEVERIDGE - GLASGOW SCRUM HALF, HAS ACHIEVED 3 CAPS FOR HIS COUNTRY

❈ BANK OF SCOTLAND

Todd Blackadder, Edinburgh Rugby. Angela Anderson, Bank of Scotland. Gary Armstrong, The Borders. Tommy Hayes, Glasgow Rugby.

❈ BANK OF SCOTLAND
PRO RUGBY CUP

giving **extra** to **Scottish sport**

The Bank of Scotland Pro Rugby Cup is played between the three Scottish professional rugby teams; The Borders, Edinburgh and Glasgow. The outcome decides their positioning in the following season's European competitions and the winner is crowned champion of Scotland.

Bank of Scotland is widely recognised as one of the largest commercial supporters of sport in Scotland. Last year more than 20,000 young people throughout the country enjoyed a wide range of sporting events and activities made possible by Bank of Scotland.

We are proud of our partnership with Scottish sport and believe our investment makes a significant contribution to the range and quality of sporting opportunities available to people in this country.

To find out more about Bank of Scotland's programme of support for sport, or the financial products and services we offer, please visit www.bankofscotland.co.uk

BANK OF SCOTLAND ❈ Always giving you extra

Then there is the new wave, the guys who have merely dipped their foot in the big-stage water or who are tipped to do so in the very near future. Amongst them are wing Mike Bartlett, full-back Stuart Moffat, stand-off Calvin Howarth, prop Lee Harrison and flanker Andrew Wilson.

When one looks at the strength and versatility of this case, it is easy to see why Glasgow made such a mighty impression in the opening weeks of the current season. Let's look more closely at the attributes and talents of three of the so-called Rookies from the Warriors line-up.

Stuart Moffat: A real sporting all rounder, he confessed: "While rugby is now my life, cricket has always been my first love." The former Edinburgh Academy pupil has wielded the willow for Edinburgh Accies, Grange, Cambridge University and Scotland.

But he kept the best until last. In his final flannelled appearance before turning pro with Glasgow, he played a star part for Cambridge in the annual Varsity match against Oxford, falling just a few runs short of a double century. It was the highest ever score by a Scot in this traditional encounter and his display earned rave reviews from all round the boundary. His appearance also meant that he had earned a double blue, having twice featured in the oval-ball version of the Varsity Match at Twickenham.

Calvin Howarth: Made the move from New Zealand to play for Boroughmuir in the BT Premiership and opted to go through the long qualification period with the aim of donning the dark blue jersey with the white thistle. This elusive playmaker that kicks goals like clockwork launched his pro career with "local rivals" Edinburgh before moving along the M8 on loan for the latter part of last season. The temporary switch became permanent and it was no surprise when Ian McGeechan included Howarth in his first provisional World Cup training squad.

Howarth, whose cousin Shane took the alternative route to Newport, had been frustrated at Edinburgh where he had to contend with hot competition for the No.10 jersey from the likes of Duncan Hodge and Gordon Ross. There was also debate among the Glasgow followers over his prospects of displacing the tried and tested Cook Islander Tommy Hayes. No problem for coach Searancke, however. He simply edged Hayes out to inside centre (or second five-eighth in his parlance) and the midfield combination has worked a treat.

Andy Hall: When the young lock received his summons to join the Scotland squad for the summer tour to Canada and the United States, he was convinced he was on the receiving end of a prank. Despite the late call-up, Hall emerged as one of the major successes of the trip, earning his maiden cap into the bargain. Now he is strongly in the running for a dream place in Ian McGeechan's World Cup plans. Hall said: "Rugby at any level is all about taking your chances when they come along. When I arrived at Glasgow from Moseley I was down at No 5 in the second row pecking order. The challenge was there for me to climb the ladder - and I just worked hard at achieving that. Touring with Scotland was far and away the highlight of my career so far - but I don't want to stop there. Having tasted the action at Test level I am hungry for more and more."

ANDY HALL - HAVING TASTED THE ACTION AT TEST LEVEL I AM HUNGRY FOR MORE AND MORE

By **DAVID KELSO** *Kelvin Media*

10 BORDERS CONTRIBUTION

DAVID FERGUSON TAKES A LOOK AT THE CONTRIBUTION THAT THE BORDERS REGION HAS MADE TO SCOTTISH RUGBY

The Borders is a swathe of lowland which, geographically, spans the south of Scotland from just two miles from Berwick-upon-Tweed in the east to Stranraer in the west.

When it comes to Scottish rugby, however, the Borders falls in line with its government boundaries. Encased in a region of under 2,000 square miles stopping halfway across the country, just to the west of Peebles, the Borders houses under 107,000 people - an average of just 23 people per square mile. The Borders is small, but with a unique richness it has represented the heartbeat of rugby union in Scotland since time began.

The Borders welcomed back its own professional team this season and though its start was less than auspicious, the crowds of several thousand - matching those Edinburgh and Glasgow have spent the last three years growing - were proof of the Borderers' enthusiasm for top-quality local rugby.

Legend has it, of course, that the famed pupil of Rugby School, William Webb-Ellis, was the 'inventor' of rugby as he scorned the rules of football by picking the ball up and running with it. There are, however, accounts the world over of previous such attempts to play a game very similar to modern rugby. Naturally, the Borders has an account of its own.

The famous 19th century writer Sir Walter Scott, who lived at Abbotsford near Galashiels, is said to have been an instigator of the rules of early football matches, where his 'Men of Ettrick' would take on the Earl of Home's 'Men of Yarrow' in 150-a-side contests.

There is an abiding story of an incident in a match at Carterhaugh where a local chap by the name of Walter Laidlaw (perhaps an ancestor of Grand Slam hero and famous Jethart son Roy?) picked up the ball and passed it wide to his teammate Walter Riddell. He, in turn, raced clear of the players and was destined to score until being caught by one of the peculiar problems of the time, a spectator on horseback, who duly ran him down. That account was written eight years before young Webb-Ellis managed his feat.

As football split into two distinct games, the Borderers took the more rugged and physical option that became rugby. Many believe this is due to the predominance of strong farmers who worked the rural southern landscape, and it has remained the number one sport ever since.

The scenic beauty of the area has not changed much since then, but working life in the Borders undoubtedly has. Gone are most of the textile mills that employed many thousands alongside the famous rivers of Tweed, Ettrick and Teviot. Many of those mills still standing are now home to flats, office complexes and telephone call centres.

The shift away from agriculture, hastened by government policy, falling demand and the foot-and-mouth epidemic of 2001, has contributed to the change, while the greater access to other leisure pursuits mean rugby clubs are no longer the same centre of Borders communities that they once were.

BRYAN REDPATH: CAPTAIN OF SCOTLAND, CAPPED 46 TIMES FOR HIS COUNTRY

60

STEPHEN CRANSTON BENEFITED FROM THE SRU'S PATHWAY SCHEME WHICH IS BREATHING NEW LIFE INTO TEENAGE RUGBY

LED BY THE INDEFATIGABLE **GARY ARMSTRONG**, THE BORDERS PROVIDES A GENUINE FOCUS FOR THOSE THRIVING IN CLUB RUGBY

On the field, the domination of Hawick, Gala and Kelso in the Scottish game are past; even the fine championship wins by Hawick in 2001 and 2002 pale against the ten triumphs of the 70s and 80s, whilst the 'Maroons' and 'Black-and-Whites' are currently in Division Two.

The upside is the improvement of clubs like Melrose and, most recently, Peebles, both of whom look set to bid for honours at the top level this season. These are different towns from the likes of Hawick and Gala, where smaller populations have a real mix of professions, and many players who work in Edinburgh and further afield.

What the Borders has increasingly had to fight against is the problem of rural depopulation and the attraction of the cities. The most recent statistics on school-leavers show that over two-thirds of people aged 18 leave the Borders altogether, mainly for work or higher education. That leaves around 35%, roughly half of which are women.

Of those remaining, many are more interested than in the early part of the 20th century in football and other sports. Some, of course, don't even care for sport. Trying to draw enough good players from the resultant figure of a few hundred to maintain the conveyor belts through the 13 senior clubs and numerous district league clubs has become immensely difficult. This may explain the increasing importation of New Zealanders, Australians and South Africans to fill the gaps in quality.

It is no wonder, then, that the Borders has struggled to maintain its influence on the national stage where its representation has dwindled from a majority to a distinct minority at all levels. For example Bryan Redpath, Gregor Townsend and Chris Paterson, were only 3 of 23 capped during the last Six Nations Championship.

The task of producing competitive teams has become greater with the introduction of a professional side, the Borders, launched in the summer of 2002. However, rather than fight the clubs for players, it has brought with it an encouraging support network aimed at helping the clubs restore the attraction of rugby and regenerate lost enthusiasm across the region.

The Borders Rugby Academy is bidding to grasp the cream of young players in the area and prepare them for the rigours of the international game, which now involves daily gym-work, weights sessions, sprints, long-distance running, and increased skills work.

With a development squad alongside, and academy systems being spawned at numerous clubs, there is a newly found optimism coming from the Borders' youth. The SRU's Pathway scheme is breathing new life into teenage rugby and creating visible ladders to the top of the game, with the Borders, led by the indefatigable Gary Armstrong, providing a genuine focus for those thriving in club rugby.

The rise of international prospects Nikki Walker, Stephen Cranston, Scott MacLeod and Ross Ford are clear examples, while Gavin Kerr and Craig Smith are other exciting Borderers playing outwith the region.

The game of rugby has changed significantly since the historic Border League was created just over 100 years ago, but, having suffered hardship on and off the field, Scotland's rugby region is beginning to see some shoots of recovery.

By **DAVID FERGUSON** Chief rugby writer for *The Scotsman*

SCOTLAND'S PLACE IN WORLD RUGBY

TODD BLACKADDER, FORMER CAPTAIN OF THE ALL-BLACKS, AND DESCRIBED BY IAN MCGEECHAN AS "ONE OF THE MOST IMPRESSIVE MEN I HAVE MET" GIVES HIS OPINION OF SCOTTISH RUGBY'S PLACE IN THE INTERNATIONAL ARENA

Sure, There have been rocky times recently, but the rugby public should realise Scotland is still a force in world terms.

Scotland's always been a pretty well-respected international side over the years, and they are always hugely welcome when they tour the big southern hemisphere countries of New Zealand, Australia and South Africa while those sides are happy to play here, too.

Remember, Murrayfield is one of the places to play Test rugby. It's got so much tradition and Scottish teams over the years have been tough to beat there - Murrayfield has that feeling you get in any of the great grounds of the world. Also, from what I've seen since arriving last year, I think Scottish rugby's on the rise. That's down to many developments including the new Borders side, Glasgow and Edinburgh posting improved results, the young guys coming through the Scottish Institute of Sport and professionalism now being firmly established in the district sides.

However, the major factor could be the Celtic League, which I think will rival the Premiership down in England as it's more colourful and the standard is just as good.

As a result, I think that the days when Scotland relied on sending a few boys down to England to be brought through are over. The players that come through the Scottish system are going to be just as good if not better and the day when, once again, a Scottish boy who has played all his rugby in Scotland becomes Test captain isn't far off.

> **I THINK SCOTTISH RUGBY'S ON THE RISE. THAT'S DOWN TO MANY DEVELOPMENTS INCLUDING THE NEW BORDERS SIDE, GLASGOW AND EDINBURGH POSTING IMPROVED RESULTS**

I SEE GUYS LIKE **SIMON TAYLOR** AND, WITHOUT EXAGGERATING, HE COULD WALK INTO ANY INTERNATIONAL TEAM IN THE WORLD

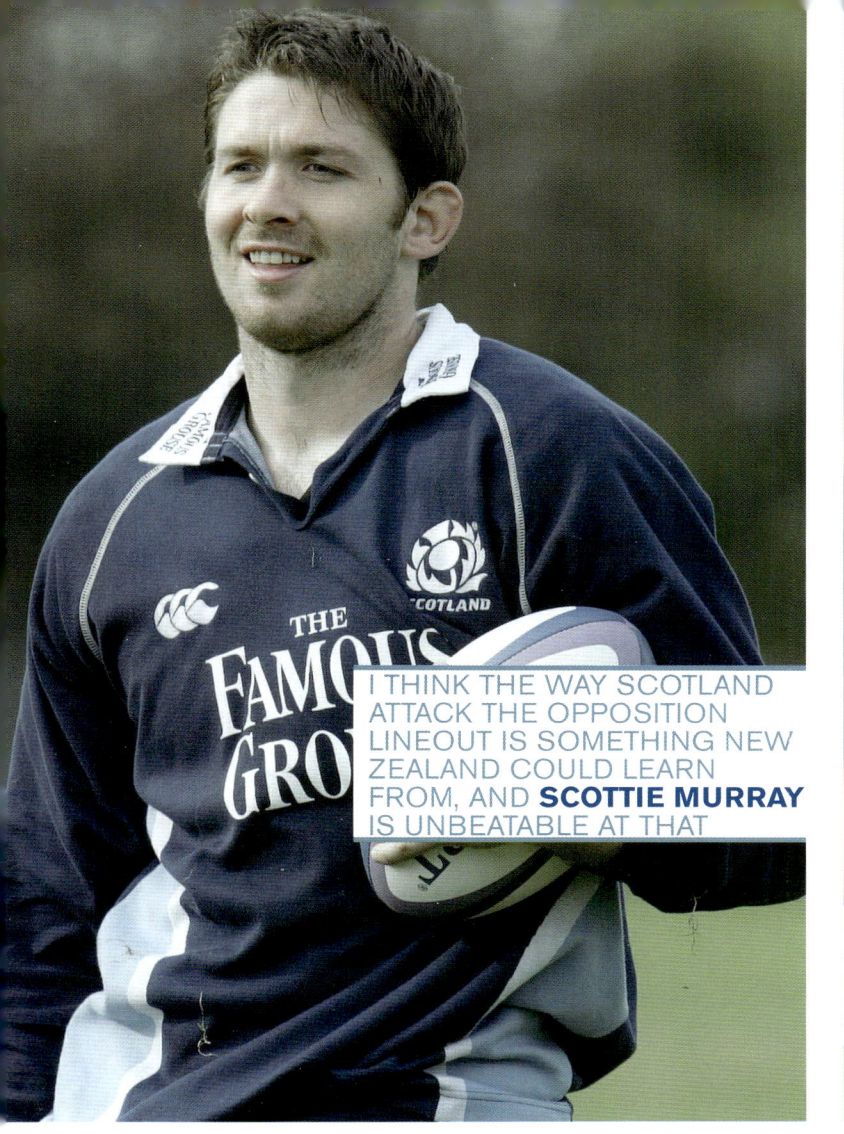

> I THINK THE WAY SCOTLAND ATTACK THE OPPOSITION LINEOUT IS SOMETHING NEW ZEALAND COULD LEARN FROM, AND **SCOTTIE MURRAY** IS UNBEATABLE AT THAT

> I DON'T THINK THERE'S ANY QUESTION ABOUT THE SCOTTISH YOUNGSTERS' COMMITMENT, WORK-RATE AND ATTITUDE... **ALLISTER HOGG** IS COMING THROUGH STRONGLY THIS YEAR

When it comes down to it, people want to go along to watch rugby and see their guys pull their jerseys on and go out there and absolutely die for the cause, and I don't think there's any question about the Scottish youngsters' commitment, work-rate and attitude. That's always been a Scottish trait and, while it's the same with boys in New Zealand, over there rugby's our number-one sport and we get access to the best coaches, technology and trainers. That environment can be duplicated here - it really can be done.

In fact, one of the most exciting things about Scottish rugby is that there are so many gains that can be made. When I was at Canterbury, to get any sort of gain you had to work so hard because we were right at the top level, whereas here you can make so much progress in a short time. The raw talent is there, we've just got to make sure that these boys come through and are able to compete.

That's why, although Scotland has a terrific reputation for coaching and Ian McGeechan and Jim Telfer command huge respect in world rugby, in actual fact the most crucial guy is the rugby coach at the Institute. He has to make sure all the young players are coming through with good work habits and rugby knowledge so the pro coaches get these guys and they're already moulded. As a result, standards will be raised all the way through.

I see the players over here as an untapped resource. You've got world-class boys here as the starting product but the challenge is to refine them and turn them into international-class players within a well-oiled machine. In that regard, I was impressed with Ally Kellock when I was involved with Scotland's Under-21s last season, and Ally Hogg's coming through strongly this year.

This season, I'm involved with the senior Scotland squad in a watching capacity. After captaining Canterbury and the All Blacks I know what a good environment is so Geech asked me to come down and look at their own environment, the messages that were being given to the players and what they were doing at training.

As a result, I can say the facilities here are world-class, second-to-none. I mean, you've got access to everything you'd ever need as far as an international set-up goes.

The quality of players is here, too, there's no doubt about that. I see guys like Simon Taylor and, without exaggerating, he could walk into any international team in the world. The All Blacks, for example, would lick their lips to get their hands on a young player like Simon. Of course, Scott Murray's in that category, too. I think the way Scotland attack the opposition lineout is something New Zealand could learn from, and Scottie is unbeatable at that. Taking all of the above into consideration, there is much to get excited about in Scottish rugby right now and I'm very pleased to be involved.

CHRIS PATERSON ON THE BREAK

DAVID FURGUSON ASSESSES EDINBRUGH RUGBY AS MAJOR CONTRIBUTOR TO THE NATIONAL SQUAD

Edinburgh's contribution to international rugby in Scotland is significant.

ALLAN JACOBSEN PASSES AN AMERICAN DEFENDER

BRENDAN LANEY

From the back row stars of Simon Taylor and Martin Leslie to the boiler-room men, Nathan Hines and Scott Murray, and prop Allan Jacobsen, to the quality backs Brendan Laney, Graeme Burns, Duncan Hodge, Chris Paterson, Derrick Lee, Graham Shiel and Craig Joiner, the capital squad has boasted a major haul of caps in recent times.

There has been a fine balance struck between experience and youthful promise, with the likes of Shiel, Joiner, Burns, Lee and Leslie providing the Test experience upon which younger players were able to lean as they found their way into professional rugby.

Laney was signed to inject instant experience to the squad, from his years as an NPC and Super 12 star with Otago and the Highlanders in New Zealand, arriving with the world-renowned Todd Blackadder. While his ability will never be seen in a Scotland jersey there is little doubting the positive effects he has had on a crop of players who currently do wear the navy blue and many destined to.

Taylor is in the vanguard of that new group of stars, with Allister Hogg, Tom Philip, Craig Smith, Mike Blair, Ali Dickson and Marcus Di Rollo among those aiming to follow him and make a mark on Test rugby.

By **DAVID FERGUSON** Chief rugby writer for *The Scotsman*

67

Always on the ball

For up-to-date full match reports

THE SCOTSMAN

Main Sponsors of:

THE BORDERS

SCOTLAND*on***SUNDAY**

Main Sponsors of:

GLASGOW RUGBY

Scotland's National Newspapers Serious About Rugby

BILL LOTHIAN SHOWS THE CONTRIBUTION THAT A UNIQUE PLAYER HAS MADE TO EDINBURGH'S RUGBY LIFE.

He's 'scored' in the company of the All-Blacks, discovered a future double British Lion in his role as talent scout and helped keep a Tongan tour on track after brokering a peace deal with the islanders' Crown Prince, and has been steward in charge of Murrayfield's royal box for the past 11 years.

If you ask George Russell what gives him the greatest buzz from rugby, the answer is simply to keep on extending a senior playing career that started 56 years ago and has been continuous ever since.

While the heart of Rugby in Edinburgh is undoubtedly Murrayfield Stadium anyone searching for the game's soul could do worse than heading to the opposite side of this great city to the Moray House club. There, 72 year old Russell is to be found training at least one night a week so that he is in shape to answer the call to turn out on the wing.

"I have managed at least one game each season for my club since 1946 and aim to continue since nothing beats playing" says the evergreen Russell who retired from his job as a health board administrator 12 years ago, adding: "While outings are fewer because of the time needed to shake off knocks I'm entitled to expect at least five seasons out of my relatively new pair of boots. Besides, if I can inspire some of those fifty-something youngsters to believe they're not too old to play I'll have served a purpose."

Russell's longevity makes him unique within the rugby community in Edinburgh (if not all of Scotland), and yet he still insists on being treated the same as any other player.

He says: "I make no allowances for my age nor ask for any. That would be totally unfair on the other 29 players and I am happy to take my chances in the knowledge that I have made it clear to my family that should anything really untoward occur responsibility lies with me alone."

What makes meeting George Russell refreshing is that he is unlike some contemporaries (and even a few a lot younger) that have found the transition to the professional game off-putting to the point of disillusionment. He retains the enthusiasm of his youth, when he wandered into the inaugural meeting of his rugby club to borrow a chair for a get-together elsewhere in the building, and was signed up on the spot! There are however some aspects of modern rugby he is particularly resistant to, such as any attempt to tamper with the traditional season. He believes the season is governed by school term times, making it impossible for fathers in particular to play through the summer with a winter shut down as some officials would like. By and large though, Russell gives the impression that every problem is solvable:

He says "I've always believed that rugby's prosperity is totally bound to the size of the base of the playing pyramid, the more youngsters that are drawn in at grass roots the greater the effect that will have all the way to the top, through greater numbers wanting to take their chance in trying to play up a level."

The need to foster these roots is why Russell will always be available for odd jobs to put back with interest what he still keeps taking out as a player. Russell has served an unbroken thirty-year stint as club president, overlapping with duties as an Edinburgh District committee member and selector from 1964-1985.

This period saw him venture along to watch Liberton FP, where he was immediately struck by the pugnacity and verve of a young full-back – the 16 year old Bruce Hay, subsequently of British Lions fame and whom Russell quickly tipped off the authorities at Scottish HQ about.

One of Russell's many roles has been as liaison officer to incoming touring sides, which has given rise to some outstanding memories, for example when New Zealand's team visited:

"Once, when assisting the All Blacks in the mid '70s I was told it was policy that once a week the entire party including myself and the bus-driver train with the team for the sake of morale. Imagine my delight when, during a touch rugby session I scored, to be greeted by a round of applause which Russ Thomas, the manager, claimed was in recognition of the first 'try' against the All Blacks on tour."

"This compared to a Tongan visit when tension arose after the Crown Prince, who was accompanying the team, felt his instructions were being ignored. The trouble was that, according to protocol, nobody could approach HRH unless invited by him to do so. I was aware there were practical reasons why the tourists could not train at 6am at a destination miles from their hotel so I put my arm around his shoulder and attempted to draw him out of the shell into which he had retreated. It worked and the tour ended with honour satisfied all round."

This could well be an example of the diplomacy that would later earn Russell a role as steward in charge of Murrayfield's Royal box for the past 11 years.

13 THE RUGBY DINNER

THE LATE GORDON BROWN - BRILLIANTLY EVOCATIVE

GENTLEMEN, PLEASE BE UPSTANDING - FRANK MORAN SALUTES A MAINSTAY OF RUGBY CLUB TRADITION.

When Rugby Union officially became a professional sport, the world changed overnight. There had always been dedicated people who gave up oodles of their time to the sport they loved but, suddenly, a door to financial reward had been opened and for those who could make it to the top, the earning potential was enticing - especially for players.

The ambitious were no longer recreation sportsmen; they were athletes who could earn their livelihood from what had hitherto been a hobby. The landscape underwent a sea change and the transformation has not been painless.

One feature however has remained constant - the rugby club dinner! Oh yes, there are now an increasing number of showpiece occasions where you are more likely to find yourself sharing a table with investment fund managers than prop forwards. Take for example the mammoth event at Holyrood Palace a year or so back when 1200 people were royally wined and dined in a vast marquee, climaxing in an auction in which items on offer included a Jack Vettriano "original print" and a Lamborghini car. These attracted noticeably few bids from even the best-heeled nouveau riche rugby stars.

Such events have their place but for the diehard rugby man, the end of season club dinner, preferably in the friendly environs of the clubhouse, is the real McCoy, accept no substitutes. The bread rolls will fly, old buffers will heckle the speakers, the captain will maintain the tradition of disclosing his colleagues' idiosyncrasies in matters of personal hygiene, and the winner of the Young Player of the Year award will continue to require the assistance of team-mates in the collection of his trophy due to the sudden collapsibility of his lower limbs. The fare is usually plain but honest although the regularity with which chocolate profiteroles feature as dessert militates against the wearing of one's Sunday best.

The pieces de resistance of the club dinner, however, are the speeches. To put it mildly, the quality varies. The president and the skipper are indispensable and predictable so the novelty value as well as the relative success of the function depends heavily on the guests. At best, a good

DAVID SOLE ELOQUENCE PERSONIFIED

GAVIN HASTINGS
OFF THE CUFF

DODDIE WEIR
PAWKY SENSE OF FUN

speaker can hallmark a dinner as one that everyone present will remember forever. When the great Willie John McBride addressed the Hawick club a decade ago, he spoke without a note for half an hour before turning to his old pal Eric Grierson, the former international referee, and inquired softly: "Mr. President, am I speaking too long?" to which the diners rose as one to respond emphatically: "NO!" They would have willingly listened all night to his vivid reminiscences shot through with wit and insight. The late Gordon Brown was another who illuminated many a club dinner by evoking quite brilliantly the experience which only the very few enjoy of taking the pitch at Murrayfield wearing a Scotland jersey.

On the other hand... I recall a dinner at which one speaker spoke at such length and to so little purpose that one diner stood on the table and threatened to douse himself with petrol before setting his clothes alight while another appeared to have hanged himself from a chandelier. At another, a well-known entertainer's gimmick was to slip surreptitiously from the room just before his turn and when announced, burst back in the guise of a Glasgow drunk. He was intercepted as he came through the door, and an over-zealous committee man (who mistook him for the genuine article) laid him out with a straight right and the words: "Private function, Jimmy."

Of course the ability to construct and deliver a good address is not given to everyone but it is clearly an enormous help to have been involved in some of the great moments of rugby history. It is difficult to make a shortlist of players with the ability to charm an after dinner audience, but here are just three of them. David Sole who led the Scots to their 1990 Grand Slam is eloquence personified while Doddie Weir's pawky sense of fun is a guarantee of happy diners. When Gavin Hastings agreed to speak at the anniversary dinner of a village cricket club, he whispered to the chap rising to address the company immediately before him, who just happened to be me, to spin it out as he had not yet prepared his material. I promptly thanked my hosts for their hospitality and, pointing out the lateness of the hour and my conviction that everyone would rather listen to Gav, promptly sat down. Since you may be reading this before the watershed, I will not repeat what he called me under his breath before delighting his audience for twenty minutes, unhampered by notes.

Over the years it has been my good fortune to attend many club dinners the length and breadth of Scotland and I can claim hand on heart to have enjoyed them all. Did I establish a record when I found myself addressing a small club function that attracted a total audience of nine? We abandoned speechifying in favour of a conversation and had a supremely convivial night. They invariably are and that is why I now invite you to charge your glasses, be upstanding, and drink a toast to the club dinner. Gentlemen, the club dinner!

By **FRANK MORAN** *The Sunday Telegraph*

MURRAYFIELD PEOPLE

SOME OF THE MANY PEOPLE RESPONSIBLE FOR ENSURING MURRAYFIELD MEETS THE DEMANDS OF THE SCOTTISH SUPPORTERS

We take a brief look at the work of some of the many people who maintain Murrayfield's status as an International venue. From greeting the visitors to fixing up the offices, together they ensure that the Scots can be proud of the home of their International team.

Nidia Stewart, Receptionist

Nidia Stewart is the first point of contact for anybody entering the SRU headquarters. All you who have met Nidia will know what an asset she is to the organisation, the epitome of the cheerful and willing receptionist, who will go to great lengths to be of help to any visitor.

However, when Nidia left her job in Peru she didn't realise that she would be standing within earshot of HRH Princess Anne one day. Her skills are often put to the test by situations as varied as the people she meets. An example of this is found as she remembers the night she had to smooth the ruffled feathers of Atomic Kitten, who were booked to perform at the stadium that night, but found themselves stranded at Edinburgh Airport with no car to pick them up. Nidia is also the friendly face who greets many of the international and Scottish players visiting the SRU. Whilst she says she likes them all and does not want to favour any player in particular she admits to naming her spaniel pup after Chris Patterson - down "Mossy"!

ALL YOU WHO HAVE MET **NIDIA STEWART** WILL KNOW WHAT AN ASSET SHE IS TO OUR ORGANISATION

Debbie Low, Merchandise Manager

The Scottish rugby store is now open for business all year round, 6 days a week and 7 days a week at Christmas time, and during Debbie Low's time as merchandise manager, the store has become one of the busiest commercial areas in Murrayfield. In a matter of only a few years, the store's turnover has risen from a mere £100,000 to over £750,000 with the aim to hit the million pound mark within the next few years. A significant part of the store's turnover comes from Scotland jerseys, and Debbie says "The most popular range in the shop has to be the replica strips, and to compliment the Canterbury range we are now introducing our own brands."

As well as a growing range of different adult strips, the store holds a large selection of branded rugby merchandise. They stock a baby range of clothes to ensure that the next generation of Scotland players are equipped for success at an early age. There are gifts and accessories for any rugby fan, from Murrayfield teddies to branded cufflinks and watches.

Last year's rugby calendar featured many favourite Scottish players. It was a big hit with the ladies who came into Debbie's store with their firm favourite being Simon Taylor. Debbie begs to differ, as she admits to preferring Duncan Hodge's photo.

Currently the store has a staff of four but on international days a large merchandising marquee is erected in the stadium and to cope with these incredibly busy periods Debbie has to find at least a further fifteen sales assistants.

TO COPE WITH INCREDIBLY BUSY PERIODS SUCH AS MATCH DAYS, **DEBBIE LOW** HAS TO FIND AT LEAST A FURTHER FIFTEEN SALES ASSISTANTS TO COPE WITH THE VAST INCREASE IN TRADE

Steve McDade, Catering Manager

When it comes to laying on a large lunch Steve's the man to ask. On international days he caters for up to 2,500 hungry diners, and provides a four-course meal and champagne for all. What's more, the meals have to be fit for a princess. To assist him in preparing these colossal feasts, Steve has 45 managers and over seven hundred staff. Whilst the vast majority of the events organised by Steve have gone swimmingly he has to admit there have been a couple of glitches. On one international day for example the gas was cut off and was only restored in the nick of time, a few hours before kick off. Then there was the occasion when all the hospitality tents blew down and replacements had to be brought up overnight, from London.

Steve has to deal with situations of a varied nature, like the visiting team from Tonga who decided everyone should get up and dance with them - just you try saying no to a 20 stone Tongan prop forward!

But his job doesn't simply stop at internationals, since the banqueting facilities that he runs are often hired out for a variety of private and public events. For example Gordon Brown announced the Scottish launch of the family tax credit in the stadium. In its time Murrayfield has also played host to international music acts such as The Eagles, The Rolling Stones and Tina Turner.

TO ASSIST HIM IN PREPARING MURRAYFIELD'S COLOSSAL FEASTS, **STEVE McDADE** HAS 45 MANAGERS AND OVER SEVEN HUNDRED STAFF

George Dent, Joiner

George Dent is Murrayfield's official joiner, but any of you who have seen him busying himself around the stadium will know that he can fix anything. Walk into any of the offices and you can't fail to see partitions and furniture that are examples of his extensive handiwork around the ground. One of his more prestigious duties comes on international match days, when it's George's job to hang the Royal pictures of the Queen, The Duke of Edinburgh and Princess Anne.

The hundreds of ramps around the stadium, in place to ensure easy and quick access to Murrayfield for those visitors in wheelchairs, are all George's work. Come rain or shine, he is on hand to assist in the smooth running of this international venue. Once, within days of a Rugby League Cup Final, the whole stadium was under up to a metre of water. George and his team had only a few days to clear up the tons of mud and debris that had accumulated, and had to enlist the assistance of private contractors and The Royal Navy. George and his team solved the problem, proving as always that the show (and the match) must go on!

This was one of the largest and most public crises that George has dealt with during his time at Murrayfield, but he is always willing to solve the smaller, but no less important problems that can arise in such a large venue. To one female supporter Murrayfield's official joiner will always be a hero. When Scotland were on the charge, she found herself locked in the lavatory. Once again, it was George to the rescue!

WALK INTO ANY MURRAYFIELD OFFICE AND YOU CAN'T FAIL TO SEE PARTITIONS AND FURNITURE THAT ARE EXAMPLES OF **GEORGE DENT'S** HANDIWORK

15 RETURN OF THE NATIVES

NATHAN HINES HAS BECOME AN ESTABLISHED PART OF SCOTTISH RUGBY

THE RETURN OF THE NATIVES - THE SCOTS WHO RETURN TO REPRESENT THEIR COUNTRY

Staging the first ever international match at Edinburgh's Raeburn Place in 1871, and contributing much to the development of the game from its early days through to the professional era, rugby in Scotland can lay claim to a proud history.

Yet right from the start, and no less so today, it has at the highest level suffered from the two basic facts that it is a minority sport played by a small nation.

Little wonder then that when it has come to seeking players for representative honours, Scottish rugby has always looked to augment its resources by casting its net beyond Scotland's shores in the quest for players who could contribute to the cause.

The involvement of exile players has over the last decade made a significant, and at times controversial impact on the Scottish game at international level, but this is hardly new.

A quick look at the roll call of capped players will show that outside Scotland two sources in particular proved fruitful to the national selectors from the first years of International rugby.

Oxford and Cambridge Universities have each produced nearly fifty players, reflecting the fact that for so long rugby was, with the exception of the Borders, the reserve of the public schools from whose number so many moved on to the two English Universities, rather than their Scottish counterparts.

An even greater supplier of players has been the London Scottish club, with around one hundred recruits to the national cause. Indeed the term 'exiles' became synonymous with players from that famous club before being widened out to refer generally to all Scottish-eligible players not based in Scotland.

As many more Scots headed south in search of employment and new opportunities, so grew the list of English clubs that could boast an international player from North of the Border. However the Scottish diaspora has been far more widespread.

The rules of the International Rugby Board state that a player can inherit eligibility from the nationality of his parents or grandparents. This has meant that a rich seam of talent is available in the former colonies where rugby has long been established and which received so many Scottish immigrants – South Africa, Australia and in particular New Zealand.

"The only difference I see between an English exile and a New Zealand exile is that the English exile speaks with an English accent, while the New Zealand exile speaks with a rugby accent." says SRU Director of Rugby Jim Telfer, more than hinting at his well-known respect for rugby in that far off land!

Brothers Martin and John Leslie, Shaun Longstaff, Gordon Simpson, Glenn Metcalfe and Brendan Laney are perhaps the best known examples of recently capped players who have come from New Zealand as descendants of Scots.

They have been joined by the likes of Robert Russell and Nathan Hines from Australia and Roland Reid from South Africa as Scotland sought to boost its competitive edge with the coming of the professional game.

Capped four times last season, Australian-born Andrew Mower is one of the most recent players to have left his native land to return to his roots, courtesy of a Scottish grandfather.

"It's probably the best decision I've ever made. Playing International rugby for Scotland was the whole reason I came over to the UK and gave up a career in banking," says Mower. "I made a lifestyle choice. I have lots of relatives here, so I feel proud to play for Scotland."

ANDREW MOWER - PLAYING INTERNATIONAL RUGBY FOR SCOTLAND WAS THE WHOLE REASON I CAME OVER TO THE UK AND GAVE UP A CAREER IN BANKING

> "WE TRY TO KEEP CONTACT WITH ALL THE CLUBS SO THAT THEY NOTIFY US OF ANY ELIGIBLE PLAYERS, THEN WE TRY AND MONITOR THEM"

There's no denying the influx of southern hemisphere players has had a major influence on Scotland's recent fortunes, but according to Telfer, for a variety of reasons it will become less significant.

"I don't think that we'll be searching now for players in New Zealand, Australia and so on," says Telfer. "I think exiles outside Britain will play a less pivotal part in the future. There will still be players coming from England however."

And it's in England that Telfer and Scotland coach Ian McGeechan are keen to foster good relations with potential Scottish players.

"The strongest links are in England because so many Scots have gone there for work, and have raised families there – I'm from that background myself!" says McGeechan. "We try to keep contact with all the clubs so that they notify us of any eligible players, then we try and monitor them. Ben Hinshelwood was like that three years ago."

In a sense Hinshelwood falls into a number of categories. Born in Australia, he is of Scottish parentage. But more specifically, his father was capped before him, and many will still remember the strong running Sandy Hinshelwood of Stewarts College FP and London Scottish, who played twenty-one times for Scotland in the late 1960s. His son Ben came over to play club rugby in England a few years ago, but, brought up on a diet of Scottish rugby, there was little doubt where his allegiance lay. "I'd always follow Scotland in the Five Nations back home in the middle of the night. "I was always supporting Scotland," he says. "I honestly didn't think I would ever play for Scotland, but when the opportunity arose, it became a real goal to do it."

Part of McGeechan's World Cup training squad for 2003, it seems more than likely that the Worcester-based player will add to the 'five-minute cap' he gained on Scotland's recent North American tour and his appearances in the 2002 Scottish Mutual Autumn Tests.

The younger Hinshelwood is just one of many being picked up in the English system, as Telfer points out. "I did a count on all the professional players, and the English exiles have produced as many pro players as the city of Glasgow for example. So it's been a very productive line for us," he says. "Simon Webster, Jon Steel and Simon Cross are very good examples of young players who have said 'I want to play for Scotland' and have come up here – and that's been their first choice," adds the SRU Rugby Director.

Despite his wishes to see as many talented Scottish-eligible players coming up to be part of the Scottish professional squads, Telfer accepts that there will also be established players who will, because of the professional rugby opportunities on offer, become self-imposed exiles and head off to England, France and elsewhere.

"If they want to go, it doesn't affect our thoughts on them," notes Telfer. "They actually can bring good things back. It's quite healthy to have players outside the country, and we've got groups of players at places like Leeds, Newcastle, Sale and Northampton."

Good news perhaps for players like Scotland forward Steve Brotherstone who took the step and headed off to France before coming back to Newcastle.

"It was just to try something different as a professional player before I finished," says the former Melrose hooker. So would he want to come back into the Scottish domestic scene? "Yes. It's improving every year. The national set-up is working hard to produce guys from the professional squads to go on and play for the International team. They're working towards the style of play so that everyone has the same idea of how Scotland is wanting to play."

Telfer's goal, when a fourth professional team is established, is to have virtually all the members of the International squads actually playing in Scotland. However it's an aspiration about which he remains realistic. "I don't think it will ever happen. Scots are natural wanderers, and there will always be some who will want to go off and seek their fortunes elsewhere."

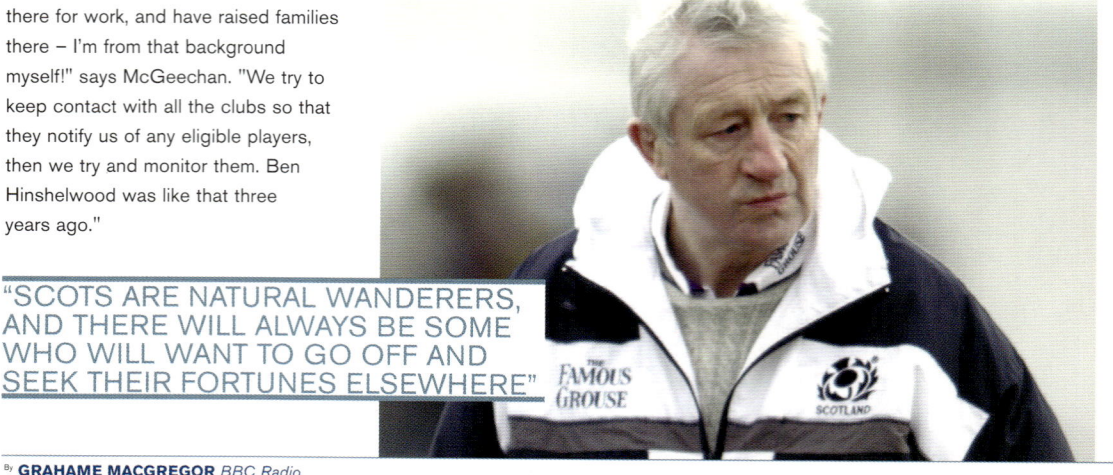

> "SCOTS ARE NATURAL WANDERERS, AND THERE WILL ALWAYS BE SOME WHO WILL WANT TO GO OFF AND SEEK THEIR FORTUNES ELSEWHERE"

By **GRAHAME MACGREGOR** *BBC Radio*

BEN HINSHELWOOD BROUGHT UP ON A DIET OF SCOTTISH RUGBY, THERE WAS LITTLE DOUBT WHERE HIS ALLEGIANCE LAY

LIFE OFF THE FIELD

WHAT SOME OF SCOTLAND'S RUGBY PLAYERS DO WHEN THEY ARE NOT PUSHING THEIR FINELY-HONED BODIES TO THE PHYSICAL LIMIT OR WRAPPING THEMSELVES AROUND SCRUM MACHINES.

Grant Robbins spoke to three well-known internationals to find out what they did in their spare time and came up with some revealing answers.

> **BUDGE POUNTNEY**, THE BATTLE-SCARRED, MARAUDING SCOTLAND AND NORTHAMPTON FLANKER, IS RUGBY'S MOST FERVENT SUPPORTER OF THE COUNTRYSIDE ALLIANCE

The undeniable success of the Countryside Alliance in mobilising a large number of people to their cause, and attracting huge media coverage, is one thing. To find out that Budge Pountney, the battle-scarred, marauding Scotland and Northampton flanker, is rugby's most fervent supporter of the Alliance, is quite another. Pountney now lives in a terraced house, half a mile from Northampton city centre but he remains a man of the soil. Last September, Pountney was doing what he does, the only thing he does when he isn't playing rugby, which was protesting at the Liberty and Livelihood march in London, proof that his heart still belongs in the countryside regardless of his postcode. His many frustrated opponents, who normally regard Budge as a ball-killing menace, would scarcely recognise the countryside rights activist speaking passionately on civil liberties.

When he is not busy inserting his battered body beneath the studs of others, the 28-year-old Pountney has carved out a new role for himself in reminding city-dwellers that social hardship and picture-postcard scenery are not mutually exclusive. He is involved in many charity events to promote the value of our rural heritage, such as the barn dance he recently organised to raise money for Moulton College's working farm, which helps urban children to see how the countryside works. Hunting is not his scene but halting the continual erosion of rural life and jobs - his father, who was a farm manager in Hampshire, was among those to be made redundant - matters a great deal. "I'm not doing it just because my father was made redundant but because of all my friends in the countryside. People have got to be allowed to do their jobs. They can't have people knocking them from the outside, saying 'You can't do that because we don't feel you should. The British countryside is a stunning place and, if the rural industries go, it won't be looked after. It'll just degenerate into a right mess. This is not just about hunting; it's the whole shebang. I would have loved to go into farming but even 20 years ago my old man was saying 'It's going nowhere, you can't afford to do this'. Instead, the boy who once enjoyed shooting and beating across the Hampshire fields around Sparsholt has now grown up to be captain of Scotland.

DUNCAN HODGE WHEN HE ISN'T PRACTISING HIS GOAL KICKING, OR PERFECTING THE LATEST THREE-QUARTER MOVEMENT, SPENDS HIS TIME MIXING POP MUSIC COMPILATIONS

You can just picture the scene. One summer many years ago, Duncan Hodge was keen to play. But he didn't want to play table tennis or Lego. What interested him lay in a dank corner of the tool shed: an ancient gramophone, with its box of 78s by Caruso, John Kirby, Harry Belafonte, etc. Scratching and whining, the wooden box made every disc sound the same; it was fun. And it was the perfect plaything, combining scientific inquiry, fresh air since it could be played outdoors, and physical exercise, as every few minutes it required a vigorous winding up. Turntables are now the toys of choice for all kinds of people. Showbiz kids dream of spinning the wheels of steel in front of an adoring crowd. These days everyone is a DJ. And Christmas is boom time for every DJ, whether superstar or supermarket shelf-stacker. Hodge, the Edinburgh and Scotland outside-half, is no exception. When he isn't practising his goal kicking, or perfecting the latest three-quarter movement, Hodge spends his time mixing pop music compilations on his mini-discman. 'It used to help keep the lads occupied on those long trips to Wales every second week,' he explains. 'I'd make up compilations - old stuff from the 60's to more popular music. Personally, I grew up on the classics: Kenny Rogers, Smokey Robinson.' So successful has Hodge become at entertaining the masses on away trips with club and country that rumour has it that Radio Forth are interested in letting him loose in their studios in the not too distant future. 'I've not heard anything officially,' laughs Hodge, dismissing any thoughts of a recording contract, 'but I don't think it's really a career option for me.'

MARTIN LESLIE 10PM ON A FRIDAY NIGHT AFTER AN EDINBURGH GAME MARTIN PUTS HIS FEET UP AND USUALLY WATCHES THE WRESTLING WHICH ALLOWS HIM TO GET AWAY FROM RUGBY FOR A WHILE

WWE wrestling, a spectacle closer to pantomime than sport in which 18-stone men in trunks pretend to beat hell out of each other (and the occasional scantily clad female), has a global following among children and teenagers. It is also a particular favourite of Martin Leslie, the strapping Edinburgh and Scotland flanker. WWE features an array of manufactured characters 'fighting' for supremacy in and out of the ring. Trading on plots that would be familiar to anyone who saw British wrestling in the 1970s, the 'competitors' play act, deploying ever more extreme stunts. WWE has expanded the genre outside the ring, weaving elements of soap opera in with the body slams and half-Nelsons while props such as chairs and sledgehammers have been used in the show. Leslie enjoys following the fortunes of his favourite wrestlers, especially a powerfully-built Samoan called the Rock, and the developments in the underlying plot in much the same way fans of soap opera do. It is, says Leslie, a moment of escapism, a chance for him to get away from the sharp end of the rugby business, to unwind and relax in front of the television. 'I usually get home well after 10pm on a Friday night after an Edinburgh game. The wrestling's always on and allows me to put my feet up and get away from rugby for a while. I especially like the ladies' - who wouldn't!

"I often invite some of the other lads to my place for a feed and then we settled down to a good night's entertainment watching the wrestling."

By **GRANT ROBBINS**

WHAT DOES IT MEAN TO BE A REFEREE?

"An uplifting experience"

"Best Seat in the House"

"Part of the Pack"

SPONSORS
D&W
DUNDAS & WILSON

GIVE IT A TRY

Iain Goodall	**Bill Calder**	**Bob Easton**	**Martyn Hawthorn**	**Roy McCombe**
Referees Manager	*R D O Borders District*	*R D O Caledonia District*	*R D O Glasgow District*	*R D O Edinburgh District*
T: 0131 346 5011 (B)	T: 01896 750044 (B)	T: 01738 620620 (B)	T: 01683 221645 (B/H)	T: 01506 409935 (B/H)
T: 0131 667 3232 (H)	T: 01896 752742 (H)	T: 01333 450818 (H)	Mob: 07764 430999	Mob: 07764 430998
Mob: 07764 178944	Mob: 07764 178926	Mob: 07764 178957	martyn.hawthorn@sru.org.uk	roy.mccombe@sru.org.uk
iain.goodall@sru.org.uk	bill.calder@sru.org.uk	bob.easton@sru.org.uk		

SCOTLAND'S YOUNG BLOODS

ALAN SHAW EXPLAINS WHY INTERNATIONAL RUGBY IS INCREASINGLY A YOUNG MAN'S GAME

Sure, you still find the odd grizzled prop grafting away at the coalface but these stalwarts of the scrum are becoming fewer and farther between as the pace, power and congested fixture lists of the modern game take their toll on some very battle-weary bodies.

So with seasons longer and careers likely to be shorter and more intense, the SRU has gone to great lengths to establish a framework in which the cream of the young rugby crop is identified early on and passed up the development path to emerge ready for Test rugby.

Progressing up through the age groups, participation in the IRB/FIRA World Junior Championship is a major milestone in the fledgling careers of our aspiring pro players.

After France, Scotland was the first of the major nations to participate in this annual Under-19s competition, making our debut in 1995. The tourney has proved to be a valuable proving ground with the number of young Scots going on to win their full caps already well into double figures including current senior XV first-choices Simon Taylor, Scott Murray, Chris Paterson and Jason White.

ALLISTER HOGG - CAPTAINED SCOTLAND UNDER 19s... AND THREE MONTHS LATER WAS ON THE BENCH FOR THE FULL SCOTLAND SIDE

21 YEAR OLD **MIKE BLAIR** TRAVELLED TO CANADA AND THE USA, AND NOW FINDS HIMSELF A MEMBER OF THE PRELIMINARY SCOTLAND 2003 WORLD CUP SQUAD

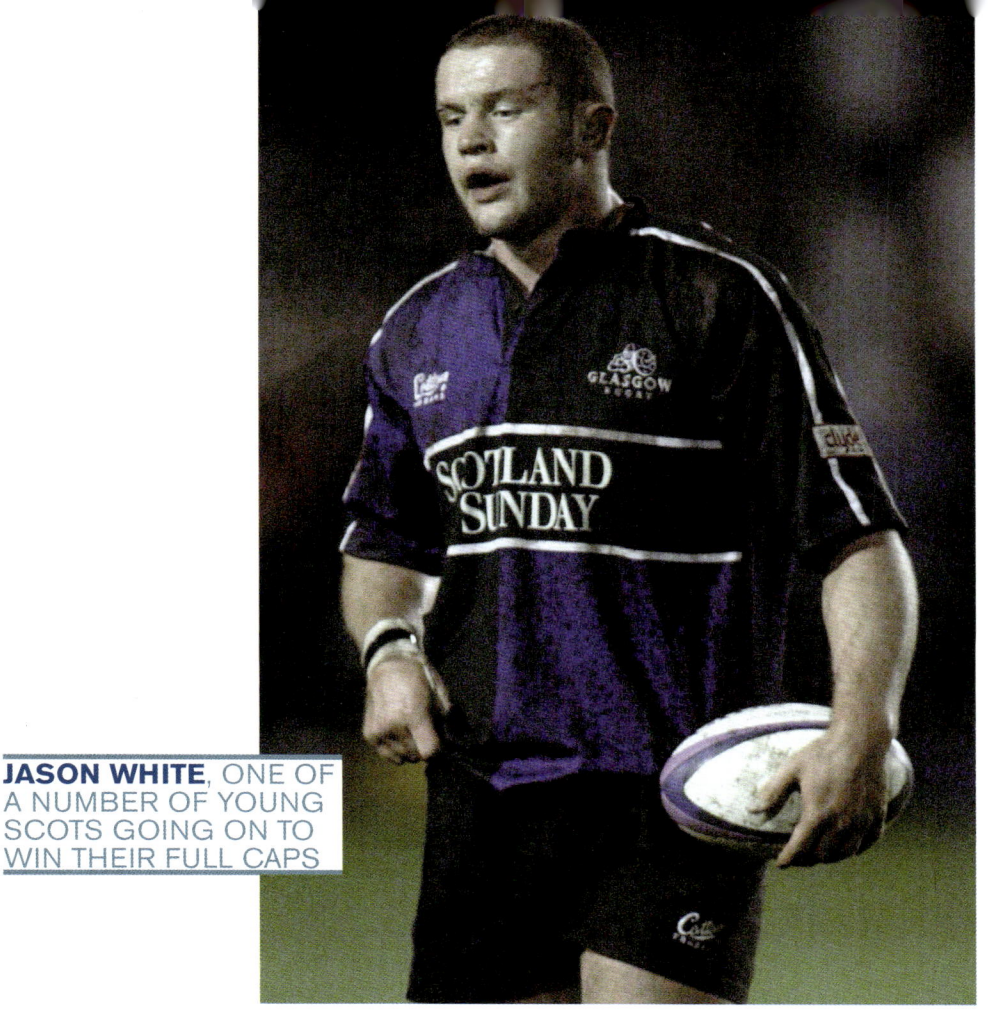

JASON WHITE, ONE OF A NUMBER OF YOUNG SCOTS GOING ON TO WIN THEIR FULL CAPS

The most recent championship, held in Italy last Easter, saw the young Scots finish a very creditable 5th after winning three of their four games. This series of successes ending with a 17-10 victory over the Auld Enemy in Treviso with a side skippered by flank forward Allister Hogg and featuring centre Tom Philip, both of whom toured North America with the full squad during the summer.

Scrum-half Mike Blair, second row Andy Hall, prop Bruce Douglas and wing Nikki Walker also travelled to Canada and the USA, and these stars of the near future have been joined by Borders centre Stephen Cranston in a preliminary World Cup training squad with an impressively low average age.

The majority of these players owe their rapid advancement in no small part to the SRU's decision to attach a number of young hopefuls to the Scottish Institute of Sport each season.

The institute was established in Stirling in 1998 to "deliver programmes and services designed to ensure top athletes progress to the highest levels". In rugby terms this means players reckoned to have the potential to reach the full Scotland XV are able to take advantage of individually tailored programmes. These highly complex programmes include coaching, sports medicine, science and psychology plus Athlete Career and Education (ACE), all taking place under the watchful eye of High Performance Coach for Rugby Bob Easson. One tartan tyro who has benefited from all of these innovations is 21-year-old Edinburgh lock Alastair Kellock who, after learning the ropes with Bishopbriggs club Allan Glen's, enjoyed two seasons and attachment to the Institute with Stirling County before signing a professional contract with the Gunners this summer.

"Glasgow to Caledonia to Edinburgh, it's been quite a journey!" smiles Alastair, who feels each stage has prepared him for the step up to the next level.

"I played all the national levels up to Under-19s at Glen's but, although I'd been there from the age of six, I had to leave if I was to keep progressing. My number-one target was to play at Stirling until I finished university and then get a contract and it's worked out perfectly.

83

"Obviously you don't know if anything's going to happen for you but I finished my MA at Glasgow and signed straight away for Edinburgh so I didn't have to get a real job!

"It was a struggle, though, fitting in uni work with training at Stirling and the Institute. I'd come out of a lecture and the last thing I'd want to do was go to the gym but that's what you have to do to achieve your goal.

"It was when I was in the FIRA squad that we heard the Institute was being set up. A few of us were called in and told we were to be attached to the Institute and I have to admit it has been brilliant for me – the two years of attachment to the Institute have prepared me for this level.

"The good thing is that, with age-group rugby and the Institute there's now a definite path to develop your career all the way from schools rugby to the pro teams.

"In fact, it's probably even more well-defined now than when I started a couple of years ago because the districts are introducing academies and back-up teams which all the Institute guys are now involved in."

While making the progression from National Division Three to Premier One to pro rugby in just two years is a big task for anyone, Alastair's taken it all in his stride – although he isn't likely to forget his rugby roots.

"I think I was lucky to start off with a club like Glen's," says the man with two tours to New Zealand under his belt already, "because when I was playing Scottish Schools I was in the first XV at the Bearyards and that gave me an edge over guys playing age-group rugby. There's quite a learning curve in National Three!

"I feel I've benefited and developed from each successive stage, however. The step up from Glen's to Stirling was similar to the one from County to Edinburgh but I'm a much, much better player now so I was able to adapt more quickly.

"There's a whole group of guys I came up through the age groups with signing for the pro teams now, like Allister Hogg and Mike Blair who are at Edinburgh, too. I've played with Mikey since Scottish Schools – he was in the first representative team I played in – and it's good to have a familiar face in the squad.

"He and 'Hoggy' have both done exceptionally well. I mean, I'm only 21 and here are guys younger than I am, in the full national set-up!

"That gives me something to aim for, though, and it's good to know that, nowadays, the selectors take the view that if you're good enough, you're old enough.

"Although I'm at Edinburgh now, I'm still learning and I couldn't have better people to learn from," the strapping second row continues. "I mean, as a lock it's fantastic to train and play alongside Scott Murray and Todd Blackadder.

"Scottie's such a talent, I'm just trying to pick up as much as possible. As for Todd, anything he says to you, you generally try and remember because it's worth keeping in mind something a former All Blacks skipper has to say.

"They make time for you and look after you which is appreciated because it's a daunting prospect coming from club rugby to the pro ranks.

"Also, I'm still attached to the Institute. We do skill sessions and enjoy the fringe benefits like the masseurs and game analysis – if Bob Easson's at any of your matches you can speak to him afterwards. Also, living in a flat in Bridge of Allan means it's just down the road so I can pop in and use the laptops at any time, which was great when I was at uni.

"Now, though, my first aim is to get a place in the Edinburgh team. I'm realistic enough to know that won't be easy with the likes of Scottie, Todd, Nathan Hines and Guy Perrett all here but I want to play international rugby and that's the next step.

"It's a gradual progression along the path but every step I've had to take I've been able to take. Even better would be to be included in the 'A' squad because training with those guys, getting your face known and learning what they're doing has got to help."

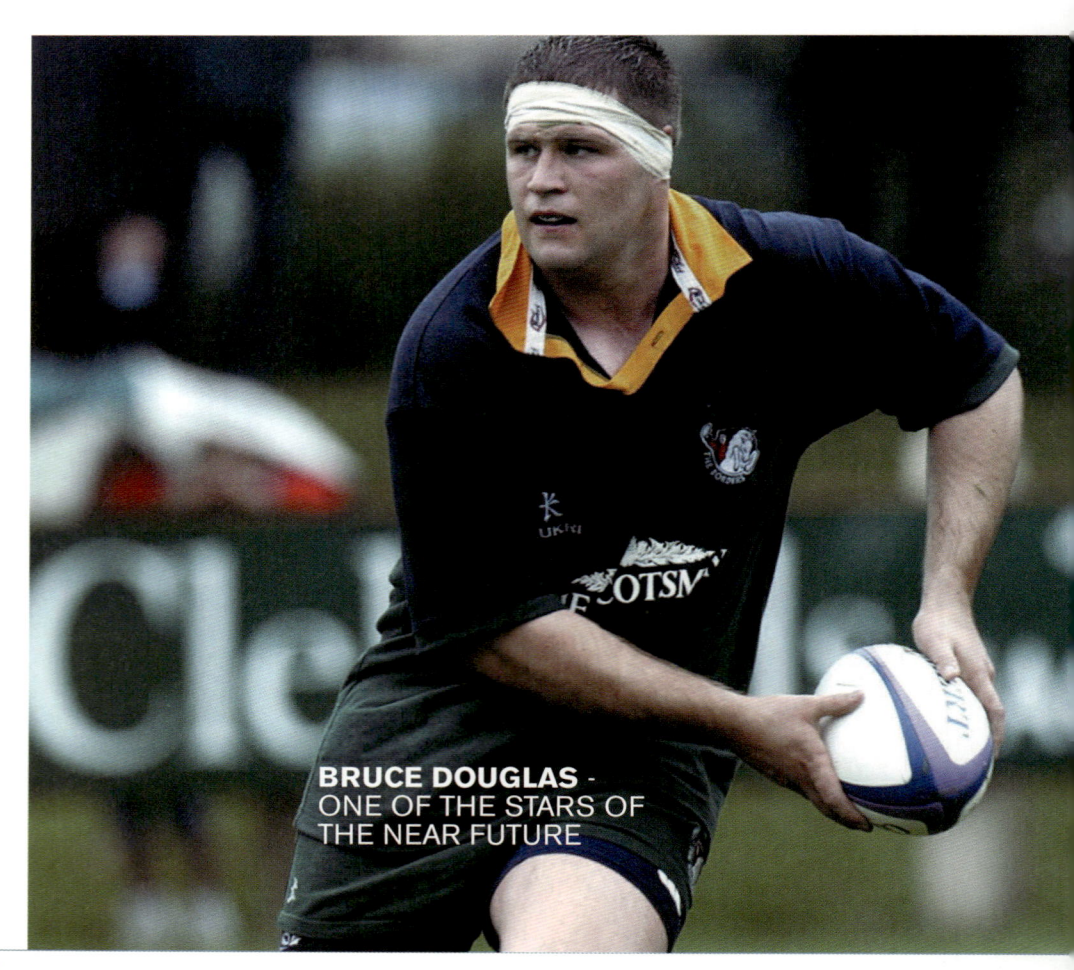

BRUCE DOUGLAS - ONE OF THE STARS OF THE NEAR FUTURE

By **ALAN SHAW** rugby writer for *The Sunday Post*

21 YEAR OLD **ALASTAIR KELLOCK**
"NOWADAYS THE SELECTORS TAKE THE VIEW THAT IF YOU ARE GOOD ENOUGH YOU'RE OLD ENOUGH"

GEORGE MACKAY PROFILES ONE OF THE MOST MISUNDERSTOOD FIGURES ON THE RUGBY PITCH – THE INTERNATIONAL REFEREE

"So, Smyth Minor", said the careers master, "you want to travel the world, see exotic places, witness exciting events and you want to be paid for doing so? You'll have to whistle for it - literally." The rugby referee, once a dejected soul drinking in the corner with only a guide dog for company, has been transformed into an international jetsetter, a glamorous figure in the glamorous world of high profile sport.

OK, not quite James Bond, but taking whistle in hand does offer a genuinely rewarding career. Among the 90 or so rugby playing countries are some of the most attractive and exciting destinations on earth. They include the South Pacific paradises of Fiji and Samoa, Caribbean idylls like Bermuda and the Bahamas, the Americas from Canada to Chile (Argentina do a particularly potent brand) all through Africa and the East and emphatically in Australia and New Zealand. Somewhere between Andorra and Zimbabwe must lie everybody's dream destination (though maybe not the latter).

And every match everywhere must have a man in the middle. It's not just a ringside seat for such epic occasions as the Springboks against the All Blacks at Ellis Park, Johannesburg, Australia v New Zealand at Sydney's Olympic Stadium, or Wales v England at the Millennium Stadium, Cardiff. The referee is right at the heart of the action, savouring the atmosphere, conducting the battle, but spared most of the big hits and the bruises. The international referee usually avoids physical trouble, but when Ireland's David McHugh was assaulted last summer by an angry South African fan many of you may have thought that there were others more deserving of a ragging than David!

Professional rugby has opened up a whole new world to the recently created occupation of professional referee. It is a supreme irony that in the year when Allan Hosie, one of Scotland's finest ever whistlers with 21 test matches to his credit, is President of the Scottish Rugby Union, no Scot is considered good enough to take charge of an international fixture.

A proud tradition that embraced Hosie and other world rated officials like Norman Sanson, Brian Anderson and Jim Fleming came to an

ALLAN HOSIE
PRESIDENT OF THE SCOTTISH RUGBY UNION WAS ONE OF SCOTLAND'S FINEST EVER WHISTLERS WITH 21 TEST MATCHES TO HIS CREDIT

TODAY'S REFEREES WILL BE INDIVIDUALLY COACHED BY THE BEST OF YESTERDAY'S MEN IN THE MIDDLE, LED BY **JIM FLEMING**, VETERAN OF THREE WORLD CUP FINALS, WHO HAS BEEN REWRITING THE COACHING MANUAL

ANDY IRELAND & MALCOLM CHANGLENG
HAVE TAKEN THE PLUNGE AND BECOME FULL-TIME REFEREES

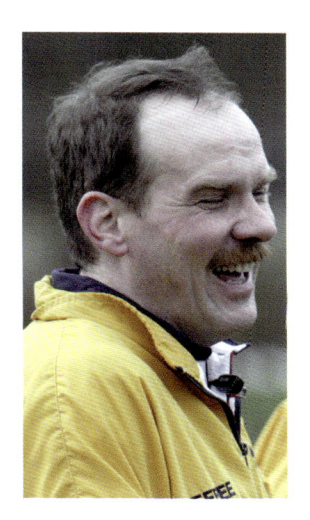

embarrassing and, hopefully, temporary halt when Rob Dickson and Ian Ramage were dropped from the elite ranks. They may have been unlucky but the new high profile pro game demands highest standards all round.

In the amateur days each country was awarded a number of international games to referee and selected the officials from their own domestic panel. Scotland were not alone in believing they had up to five men capable of handling international games at one time. The distinction of breaking up this cosy cartel goes to a Scot.

It is best our hero remain anonymous to spare the blushes of the good folk of a certain Border town. It was after he had taken a match between Australia and New Zealand that, promoted by the Australians (who do a sense of grievance very well) a new system of merit-based selection was instituted, with the International Rugby Board doing the choosing.

Now there is an A list who handle the very biggest games - Tri nations, Six Nations, World Cup Finals - and a B list who take charge of a still extensive range of other internationals, including World Cup qualifiers. If your name is not on either list you don't referee international rugby, full stop.

Right now the Scots are out of the loop, and so the Scottish Rugby Union has launched a major campaign to put it right. Rugby World Cup 2003 has already been written off - it's too late to get our men there. But the aim is to have two or three Scots in the line-up for the 2007 event and more if possible in the decade ahead.

A core of professional referees has been recruited, mostly part-time on a retainer and match fee. Two, Andy Ireland, a 38-year-old prison officer from Grangemouth, and Malcolm Changleng, a 31-year-old former Gala three-quarter, have taken the plunge and gone full time. They will spearhead the drive, but theirs is no easy option.

To get onto even the B list they have to achieve 10 assessments of 86 or better in selected games of European Cup or higher level. They also have to prove their physical fitness to rigorous standards set by the IB. Long gone are the days when Mr D. G. Walters would referee the Varsity Match at Twickenham smartly attired in his club blazer. Pro players are bigger, fitter, faster and refs are expected to keep up with them. Former fitness advisor to the national squad, David McLean, will make sure they are up to the job.

The Scots have taken the radical step of throwing out the old assessor system, which drove a huge wedge between the refs and the players, who felt they were more concerned with showing how well they knew the laws than with the spirit of the game. Now, today's referees will be individually coached by the best of yesterday's men in the middle, led by Jim Fleming, veteran of three World Cup Finals, who has been rewriting the coaching manual.

Iain Goodall, the SRU official charged with implementing Scotland's brave new policy, stressed "What we are seeking is a change of culture. The professional referees will be working with our professional teams, coaching players in the applications of the Laws, and will work with the national teams in the same areas. We are looking to replace them-and-us attitudes with harmony and understanding to produce a better, faster, freer game. But the players must play their part".

The decision to opt for neutral referees in Celtic League games widened the horizons for Scottish referees, giving them regular exposure to the game in Wales and Ireland, and the expansion of Heineken Cup and Parker Pen games has spread that experience to England and the Continent. The Scots have also initiated an exchange system with France, a memorable experience for Malcolm Changleng when he found waving yellow cards about did rien to stop the traditional violence. "Welcome to real French rugby, mon ami."

In the past referees were drawn from the ranks of retired players and while this is still a well trodden path to the middle, like a player, a referee has to start young if he is aiming to scale the heights. As Iain Goodall says "If we are to get referees up to international standard, we want them to start in their mid 20s. It takes about 10 years, but people with exceptional qualities will be fast tracked. Although referees will not make the kind of money paid to top players, they will not go short, they will travel in style and they will be around for a good spell."

The ladder is being put in place for the referees of the day-after-tomorrow with a licensing system which means every match in Scotland is now handled by a licensed referee and coaching is already going on in schools to turn pupils into referees at their own level. There are mature students too. Kenny Milne, a Scotland and British Lions hooker of recent vintage, recently went, with Andy Irvine, through a basic refereeing course. "Every player should be made to go through a level 1 course so they understand the laws they are trying to play to", the bold Kenny declared, presumably having appeared 40 times on the international field in a fog of uncertainty.

Another ex-player on the course insisted that he would never shout at the referee again. Surely that's taking it a bit too far. You pays your money and you hurls your abuse. Even if today's professional referees are better prepared, fitter and more sympathetic to the spirit of the game somebody has to play the scapegoat, and he knows they don't really mean it, do they?

By **GEORGE MACKAY** *The Mail on Sunday*

SCOTTISH RUGBY'S LONG AND RICH HISTORY, PRESERVED AT MURRAYFIELD FOREVER

From hundred year old rugby strips to last year's press cuttings - Here we take a look at just a few of the treasures of memorabilia to be found in the Murrayfield archives. The very birth of the game as we know it is chronicled there, with items stretching back into the mists of time. The numerous changes to the game in its long and varied history are also to be seen, as these images from the past and present show…

Whether you have a query about Scottish match programmes from 1900 or need to track down press cuttings on a Scotland match from last year, Fiona White is the person to contact. She fields a huge variety of requests for information and artefacts from Scottish rugby's rich history, as well as coordinating the public's guided tours of historic Murrayfield.

Requests for data come from a range of sources, both private and public. Fiona deals with all information enquiries, from requests for input on research projects to enquiries from the families and fans of Scotland players past and present. Since she is in charge of a huge archive of material, she is often able to provide exactly the items and information that people are looking for. There is a treasure trove of Scottish rugby memorabilia under her care, with items such as original match balls, team photographs, programmes and even dinner menus, all ranging from the late 1800s right up to the present day. Items that each have a long story, some of glory and victory, and some with a less happy (but no less interesting) story attached!

As well as historical information, Fiona keeps a detailed current record of how today's Scotland team is progressing in the eyes of the media. She updates comprehensive files on the careers of all Scottish International players with press information, adding daily to an ever-growing archive that reaches back over many years.

That archive is also growing at a great pace, as Fiona often receives offers for new donations to the collection on top of the ongoing press updates that she carries out personally. Here's hoping that this time next year she will be cataloguing a vintage year for Scottish successes!

WALES VS. SCOTLAND PROGRAMME, FEBRUARY 2ND 1907

Having recently beaten England, Wales came to this match full of confidence in their formation of seven forwards. However, a solid Scottish defence was combined with a pack so eager that they had one try disallowed for being offside. This tendency to push too far during the Scottish attacks meant that the only score in the first half was due to an offside penalty conceded by the exuberant Scots' pack. Players of note in the game included D.G. MacGregor, a player making his International debut who had a claim to both Welsh and Scottish nationality, who was actually considered for the Welsh reserves but chose to play for Scotland on the day. The pressure was kept up on the Welsh defensive line throughout, and finally this paid off as A.B.H.L Purves was able to fend off H.T. Maddocks and score in the corner. The try was not converted leaving the final scoreline at 6-3 to the Scots.

HISTORY OF THE HANDBA GAMES

There are many contenders for the title of the forerunner of Rugby Football as we know it, but in Scotland the Border Ba' games encouraged a love of ball games that has endured right up to the present day.

The Ba' games are believed to have developed from a game called Harpastum, imported by the invading Romans in the early years of this millennium, in which two teams competed on a rectangular pitch to get a small ball across the opposing team's line. There is a possibility that this ancient sport influenced the birth of the Border Ba' games, since the main Roman road into Scotland runs past Jedburgh, and ends near Melrose (where, incidentally, Rugby sevens was born many hundreds of years later). The fact that many of these Border communities were exposed to the Roman game for over 100 years does suggest that the handba' games might be rooted in an even earlier sport.

The Ba' games themselves were played regularly in Borders towns and villages, several hundred years before the day in 1823 when William Webb-Ellis picked up the football and ran with it at Rugby school, to help form the game we know today. Despite the game forming one of the roots of modern rugby, many of the rules were very different from those of our modern game. There was no fixed time limit on the proceedings, with handba' games often lasting several hours. Further, the 'pitch' was huge, with the village or town's fields and streets forming the play area. Two teams of unlimited size were involved, the object being to get hold of the ba'. These teams were often divided into two areas of the same town, with an example of this being found in Jedburgh, where the two teams are the 'uppies' and the 'doonies'. The ba' itself was a small, hard leather sphere about the size of a modern tennis ball, and once it was obtained, had to be carried to an agreed point in the opposing side's area of play.

It was not that simple to obtain the ba', however. As the rules of the game were, to say the least, freeform in nature, the application of brute force was the key to victory. The kicking of the ba' was probably not a feature of the game, as the kicker might expect to sustain serious injuries in the giant scrums that ensued in the chase. Whilst the playing of Borders handba' declined eventually, it is still played occasionally, such as the annual match at Jedburgh, and is a reminder of the roots of the game we see played today.

ORIGINAL EXAMPLES OF THE BALLS USED IN HANDBA' GAMES IN THE BORDERS

SCOTLAND VS. ENGLAND
RAEBURN PLACE 13TH MARCH 1886 - DESPITE THE GREAT EFFORT BEING PUT IN BY THE SCOTTISH FORWARDS, THE MATCH ENDED IN A SCORELESS DRAW.
PAINTING BY W.H. OVEREND AND L.P. SMYTHE

The painting above was created by W.H Overend and L.P. Smythe, and copies of the painting still hang at Murrayfield and Raeburn Place today. It depicts the 1886 Scotland-England match at Raeburn Place, which took place on the 13th of March. Despite the bitterly cold weather, the attendance at the match was very high, and special trains had to be laid on to ferry the spectators to and from the International. The match was also the first ever Rugby international to have mounted police in attendance, as can be seen in the painting, in the background to the left of the referee. Although the game ended in a 0-0 draw, it was a hotly contested match that Scotland dominated for the first three-quarters of the match, with an English fight-back at the finish. The Scots had several near-misses on the try line with R.H Morrison (Edinburgh Univ.) knocked into touch just before his score, and G. Wilson (RHFSP) having his try disallowed since he was judged to have knocked on the ball when he caught the pass that allowed him to touch down. Charles Reid (Edinburgh Acad.) also had a missed chance at a score, and is pictured above in the right foreground.

SCOTLAND - J.P. Veitch (RHSFP); W.F. Holms (RIEC), G.R. Wilson (RHSFP); R.H. Morrison (Edinburgh Univ.); A.R. Don Wanchope (Fet.-Lor); A.G.G. Asher (Fet.-Lor, Edinburgh Wrs); J.B. Brown (Glasgow Acad.); A.T. Clay (Edinburgh Acads.); T.W. Irvine (Edinburgh Acads.); M.C. McEwan (Edinburgh Acads.); D.A. Macleod (Glasgow Univ.); C.J.B. Milne (West of Scotland); C. Reid (Edinburgh Acads.); J. Tod (Watsonians); W.A. Walls (Glasgow Acads.)

ENGLAND - C.H Sample (Durham); A.E. Stoddart (Blackheath); R. Robertshaw (Bradford); E.B Brutton (Cambridge University); A. Rotheram (Richmond); F. Bonsor (Bradford); W.G. Clibborn (Richmond); C. Gurdon (Richmond); E.T. Gurdon (Richmond); R.E. Inglis (Blackheath), G.L. Jeffery (Cambridge Univ.); C.J.B Marriott (Blackheath); N. Spurling (Blackheath); A. Teggin (Broughton Rangers); E. Wilkinson (Bradford)

REFEREE - H. Cook (Ireland) **TOUCH JUDGES** - J.S. Carrick, G.Rowland Hill

SCOTLAND VS. FRANCE PROGRAMME
24TH JANUARY 1925

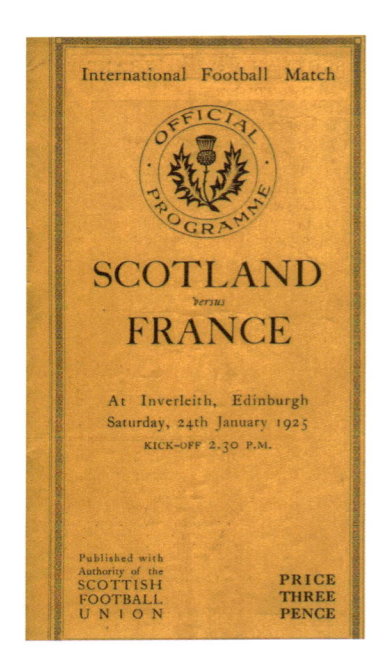

The second half of this match was played as a partial eclipse of the sun reached its zenith. The solar eclipse did not affect play, however, nor did it prevent I.S. Smith (Oxford University) from scoring four tries throughout the match. This game was also notable as the last International match to be played at the Inverleith ground before Scottish rugby moved to Murrayfield. 20,000 fans turned out to see Scotland outscore the French team by a considerable margin. Despite the impressive scoreline, some criticisms were made about the strength and confidence of the Scottish scrum, which did not dominate as some viewers would have liked.

THROUGH THE TURNSTILES -
HOW TICKETS HAVE CHANGED IN THE LAST CENTURY

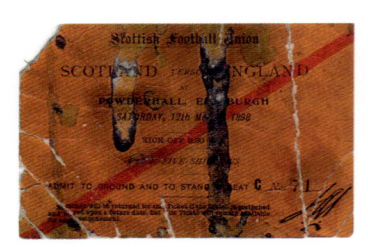

Scotland vs. England 1898 **Scotland vs. England 1925** **Scotland vs. England 1990**

A selection of the tickets contained within the Murrayfield archives in Edinburgh. Whilst the appearance and price of the tickets has changed over the many years of Scottish rugby, the passion and devotion of Scottish rugby fans has not. From left to right, the 1898 match ended in a 3-3 draw at Powderhall, which was used as the Inverleith ground was not finished in time. The 1925 Test at Murrayfield ended in a great 14-11 win for Scotland, although the lead changed hands no less than three times during the match, which was watched by 70,000 rugby fans. 1990 saw a classic victory for Scotland, as they beat England 13-7 to claim the Five Nations, Calcutta Cup and Grand Slam in one fell swoop.

SCOTLAND JERSEY AND CAP, 1874

THE HISTORY OF THE THISTLE - SCOTTISH KIT FROM PAST TO PRESENT

A classical, oft-told story of Scottish rugby is of how, when the SRU secretary was handing out the Scotland jerseys to the players in the first match after the First World War, Jock Wemyss asked where his was. "You got one before the war," barked the official.

Not, in fairness, that the SRU were alone in practising such parsimony in the name of amateurism. Carson Catcheside, the England wing, who, in 1924, scored one try or more in each of the four matches of an England Grand Slam, charged three pounds for his return rail fare from Newcastle. He got his expenses but with the fare amended by the Rugby Football Union to two pounds, 19 shillings and eleven pence. Catcheside took due note and the next time itemised the cost in question: Rail fare £2 19s 11d. Toilet 1d. The oldest Scotland jersey in the SRU's possession dates back to 1877 and belonged to West of Scotland's Henry Melville Napier, a product of Glasgow High School who was renowned as "a grand scrummager and excellent dribbler." The SRU have his cap, which has also lasted well and is not too different from the cap a player receives today. In the early years, Scotland teams wore knickerbockers but they gave way in the 1880s to what an earlier SRU historian, the late Sandy Thorburn, termed 'Long shorts'. Henry Melville Napier's jersey is still in very good condition today, the button on the back of the neck puzzling SRU historian Fiona White, until she found a reference in the old SRU library and Museum brochure. This revealed that, astonishingly enough, the side used to don a white collar and black bow-tie for the pre-match team photograph!

There was also a time when a Scotland player who swapped his jersey for an opponent's had to replace it at his own expense. Mercifully, that stricture was eventually jettisoned. The famous thistle has always adorned the Scotland jersey save, strangely for the plain white jerseys in which, in the Victory international of 1946, Scotland played so memorably to become the only country to beat the touring Kiwis, the decidedly formidable New Zealand Army XV. These days, however, Scotland have revamped their kit, including a large range of leisure wear. Having taken soundings from both their players and supporters, they have shed the purple from their rugby jerseys, and in this professional era, the latest strip is very different from the jersey of old that Henry Melville Napier wore in 1877.

THE SCOTLAND WOMENS TEAM MAKE HISTORY AT MURRAYFIELD AS THEY TAKE THE PITCH

MAKING HISTORY AT MURRAYFIELD AS THE SCOTLAND WOMEN'S RUGBY TEAM BECOMES THE FIRST NORTHERN HEMISPHERE WOMEN'S SIDE TO PLAY A TEST IN THEIR NATIONAL STADIUM

Women's First International Test at Murrayfield

Murrayfield Stadium on 24 November 2002 saw Scotland's National Women's team become the first female national rugby team in the northern hemisphere to play in their National rugby stadium. The team certainly rose to the big occasion with an impressive win over Sweden.

Scotland's Women drew first blood in this historic first international after a prolonged period of pressure, when the Scots at last managed to put width on the ball and worked it right for debutant Sharon Brodie (East Lothian), a sports science student at Telford College in Edinburgh, to cross for an unconverted try. The Swedes' response saw left wing Cecilia Lundin pull back three points with a penalty that sneaked in off the left-hand upright.

Scotland made a change early in the second-half, Alison Newall (Clifton) replacing Gill Gibbon (Royal High) at scrum-half and extended their lead five minutes into the second period when they worked the ball left for stand-off Sara Mears to release Angela Hutt (Murrayfield Wanderers) for their second try.

Sweden's persistent ball-killing incurred the wrath of English referee Sean Davey who sent Frida Ryberg to the sin-bin after seven minutes of the half. Scotland quickly took advantage as Brodie showed her pace romping in for her second score from 30 metres. Brodie was involved in Scotland's fourth try too, keeping the ball alive as she stepped in from close to the right touchline to give the scoring pass to supporting No 8 Donna Kennedy (Royal High).

Attention had focused on the debutants in the Scotland side but Rimma Petlevannaia (Murrayfield Wanderers), winning her 50th cap, was determined to enjoy some of the limelight, intercepting on the Swedes' 10-metre line in the 60th minute and striding in for the Scots' fifth try, to which she added the conversion.

The Scots rounded off the game with a well-worked try in injury time by replacement Haley Campbell on her debut, making the final score Scotland 34 Sweden 3.

HALEY CAMPBELL HANDS OFF THE SWEDISH DEFENCE ON THE WAY TO SCORING THE DEBUT TRY

RHONA SHEPPARD RELEASES THE BALL

SHARON BRODIE MAKES AN IMPRESSION AT MURRAYFIELD WITH HER FIRST CAP FOR SCOTLAND

WOMEN'S SIX NATIONS 2002-03

MARY PAT TIERNEY AND DONNA KENNEDY

The women's fixture dates are played the same weekends as the men. The only exception to this is that the sixth side in the women's Six Nations game is Spain instead of Italy.

SIX NATIONS MATCHES

SATURDAY 15 FEBRUARY	vs	IRELAND	AT MEADOWBANK STADIUM K.O 14:00
SATURDAY 22 FEBRUARY	vs	FRANCE	AT EVREUX K.O TBC
SUNDAY 9 MARCH	vs	WALES	AT MEADOWBANK STADIUM K.O 14:00
SATURDAY 22 MARCH	vs	ENGLAND	AT THE STOOP K.O TBC
SATURDAY 29 MARCH	vs	SPAIN	AT MEADOWBANK STADIUM K.O 12:00

BEFORE MANY NORTHERN HEMISPHERE TEAMS, SCOTLAND HEADED SOUTH, IN A TALE OF FEARSOME BEATINGS AND HUGE STRIDES FORWARD

New Zealand rugby does not merely seethe with rumour, it lives for it. Anecdotes are exchanged like match tickets, the link between the dreaming thousands and their rugby gods - and few stories are better than the one about Ian McGeechan and a middle-aged Wellington woman.

Two days after Scotland had eked out a 20-all draw with France in the 1987 World Cup, Ian McGeechan and Scotland selector Derrick Grant had driven into the town before the next game against Zimbabwe and stopped at the first coffee shop they found. Here they encountered a local woman seated at the next table. She immediately recognised the pair and began analysing Scotland's options.

"She started talking about our game, how it was the best match of the World Cup so far," McGeechan recalls, a grin creeping from the edge of his lips. "Why didn't we put more pressure on their tight-head?" she asked. "Why hadn't we driven from the back of the line-out ...the French were vulnerable there. And could we not have worked our back-row more into the game because France were a bit slow in that department?"

McGeechan and Grant looked at one another in bewilderment. "We could have gone to any clubhouse in Scotland and not had that conversation," says McGeechan. "We were pretty anonymous at home as rugby players, but 12,000 miles away, someone off the streets had recognised us. I wondered, 'If that's the mother of a New Zealand rugby player, just what an environment to be living in?'"

McGeechan, in his second tenure as the Scotland head coach, is a self-confessed junkie of southern hemisphere rugby. Observing him in his Murrayfield office, the inevitable paperwork clogging his desk, it is easy to see why such a dynamic umbilical cord exists between McGeechan, a veteran of several British Lions tours, both as a player and coach, and the south.

His is an all-encompassing, universal passion. 'I've been strongly influenced by the southern hemisphere, ever since 1974 when I first went to South Africa as a player,' says McGeechan. "The toughest competitive rugby I've played was in the southern hemisphere. You couldn't get away from the fact that rugby was the No.1 sport in New Zealand and South Africa. The environment in which the southern hemisphere players operated, and how seriously they trained, was always in the back of my mind. It definitely affected my competitive edge. I've carried that into my coaching.

"The best Scotland tour I've ever been on was in 1990 to New Zealand. We nearly beat the All Blacks in the second Test and gave them a hell of a fright in the first. We got ourselves tactically, technically, attitude-wise spot on. Our young players are hitting an environment now which is akin to the southern hemisphere. They have the ambition to be professional rugby players.

"Professionalism has nothing to do with being paid and everything to do with attitude. The only thing that could affect us is the structure of the season and we've got what we wanted - the leading players taking part in no more than 30 games - almost by default."

Nevertheless, there is enough for the national coach to worry about, but he seems unfazed. "We've started to get the buzz back into Scottish rugby, because, if you like, the mist is clearing," he says. "You can see from the robust system that's developing there are benefits to our clubs and benefits to the top end of the game. There is a really strong skeleton in Scottish rugby around which everything can work."

Amid the growing hegemony of the southern hemisphere and the giant strides England and France have made since the game went professional in 1995, McGeechan was, of course, embroiled in the turmoil of the English game as coach of Northampton at the time. A hands-on doer, he could see the way forward. "In the 80's we spoke about how we could keep our players ambitious. It was a stated objective to go to the southern hemisphere as often as possible.

> 'THE TOUGHEST COMPETITIVE RUGBY I'VE PLAYED WAS IN THE SOUTHERN HEMISPHERE. THE ENVIRONMENT IN WHICH THE PLAYERS OPERATED AND HOW SERIOUSLY THEY TRAINED...
> ...DEFINITELY AFFECTED MY COMPETITIVE EDGE. I'VE CARRIED THAT INTO MY COACHING.'

"So, when no other country was going south, we went to New Zealand in particular, time and time again. We took some fearsome beatings down the line, but actually our top group of players all made huge strides forwards. It was significant that all those players were exposed to southern hemisphere rugby.

"I know what sort of rugby can be effective for Scotland," adds McGeechan. "Australia's set-up is the closest to ours because they have problems of size and threats from other sports. We're similar to New Zealanders in our characteristics. Although we've been heavily influenced by the southern hemisphere, one of the reasons Scotland's stayed competitive is that we haven't copied anybody in the way we play."

Sean Lineen, the former Scotland centre, thinks the Scottish Rugby Union's policy of importing foreign players has been a stimulus to these parts. Lineen, who arrived from Auckland in October 1988 and in three months made his Scotland debut, against Wales in the Five Nations, explains.

"They've brought the likes of Todd Blackadder, the former All Black captain, to Scotland. We've already seen the positive rub-off effect that's

By **GRANT ROBBINS**

had on Edinburgh," says Lineen, who is now coaching Scotland's Under-21 backs. 'I, too, became a better player, mentally and physically, in Scotland. I now regularly work with the next generation in my new role with the SRU. There's a lot of good youngsters coming through the system.

"I don't see the real benefits now that there once were," says Finlay Calder, Scotland's successful Lions captain who secured a rare series victory over Australia in 1989. "In the past, tours down south were used as early preparation for the new season, a chance for coaches to assess the players' form and fitness. They knew that if a player coped with the southern hemisphere, they'd cope with the Five Nations.

"Now, our players play so many games, at such intensity, that needless tours to the southern hemisphere are in danger of exposing them to burnout. We've seen the benefits to players who were rested over the summer, but they can still be useful as a vehicle for development."

I wander away from Murrayfield, eventually. A small boy is wearing an All Black shirt, with No. 11 on the back. He lopes like Jonah Lomu. Nearby, a man of about 60 chatters away. He, too, is wearing a rugby shirt, that of the Springboks. The next joust for Scotland with the southern hemisphere, it seems, is never very far away. Players to replace those they've lost.

Using IT to convert all the action into analysis

Computacenter is the official data and statistics partner of the Royal Bank of Scotland Six Nations Championship.

Our aim – to bring a new level of insight to the game through the innovative use of IT.

Working with top grade international referees, we track the action as it happens.

Quick feed – detailed reports are distributed after the final whistle to the media and team coaches.

From comprehensive match analysis to individual player performance, we provide the facts that support the game.

Leading UK organisations work with Computacenter to raise their game. Why not join them?

IT infrastructure services that consistently deliver

Log on to **www.computacenter.com/rugby** for all the official match statistics

computacenter

Official data and statistics partner of the RBS Six Nations Championship

22 THE CALCUTTA CUP

ANDY NICOL TRIUMPHANTLY HOISTS THE CALCUTTA CUP AFTER THE WIN AGAINST ENGLAND IN 2000

ALAN EVANS LOOKS AT THE HISTORY OF THE WORLD'S OLDEST RUGBY UNION TROPHY

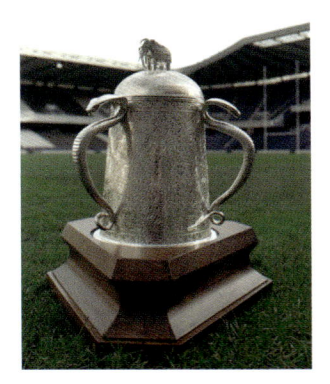

The Calcutta Cup
Presented to the Rugby Football Union
by the Calcutta Football Club
as an International Challenge Cup

To be played for annually by England and Scotland
1878

The years have gone by, 125 of them in fact, since the Calcutta Football Club of India offered to the Rugby Football Union in England a unique trophy to be competed for every season. It was – and is – the most famous rugby union trophy anywhere in the world, famed as a magnificent example of Indian craftsmanship, made of rupees withdrawn from the bank and featuring three snake handles and an elephant mounted on its lid.

England's President in 1877, Mr A G Guillemard wrote back to Mr G A J Rothney in the sub-continent that

"The Committee accept with very great pleasure your generous offer of the Cup as an International Challenge Cup to be played for annually by England and Scotland – the cup remaining the property of the Rugby Football Union."

On 10 March 1879 a record crowd of 10,000 duly assembled at Raeburn Place for the first-ever Calcutta Cup match. It ended in a draw – a drop goal for Scotland and a converted try for England. Scotland won the Cup for the first time three years later, winning by two tries to nil in Manchester.

Since then there have been many great encounters. Scotland won the first-ever international at Murrayfield in 1925, with a Grand Slam as a bonus, and completed an historic double by winning for the first time at Twickenham the following year. Don't mention 1990 to the men in white but that was another great Murrayfield occasion and Calcutta Cup triumph. Or 2000. Or... well, there are sure to be many more famous wins in the future.

FACTFILE

Since 1879 there have been 109 Calcutta Cup matches. Scotland have won 37, England 58 and 14 matches have been drawn. Scotland's biggest margin of victory was at Murrayfield in 1986 when they won 33-6.

By **ALAN EVANS** Cardiff RFC

23 OUR SONG

IT HAS BEEN PLAYED SLOWLY, AND WITH AN OVER-EXCITED QUICK TEMPO, BUT NO MATTER THE BEAT O FLOWER OF SCOTLAND REMAINS A POWERFUL ANTHEM UNIQUELY ASSOCIATED WITH SCOTTISH RUGBY

RONNIE BROWNE SINGING O FLOWER OF SCOTLAND.

O FLOWER OF SCOTLAND

O Flower of Scotland
When will we see your like again
That fought and died for
Your wee bit hill and glen
And stood against him
Proud Edward's army
And sent him homeward
Tae think again

Those days are past now
And in the past they must remain
But we can still rise now
And be the nation again
That stood against him
Proud Edward's army
And sent him homeward
Tae think again

Younger supporters of the Scotland side might be forgiven for believing it has been part of the national team's identity since the 19th century, such is its traditional, distinctive sound, but, in fact, it has only been used as the national anthem for 13 years.

The ballad was written in the late 60s by the late Roy Williamson, one half of the popular Scottish folk group The Corries, and after becoming a part of Scottish culture was first officially sung as the rugby team's anthem, at the request of the then captain David Sole, before Scotland's autumn match against Fiji in 1989 then during the 1990 Five Nations Championship - it proved a lucky choice as the season ended with Scotland's last Grand Slam.

Sole recalled: "It was nice to have a song that the players could sing and one that the crowd reacted to as well."

Williamson's singing partner Ronnie Browne, now retired, recalls the feeling of pride the singing duo felt when the Scottish Rugby Union approached the pair and asked if it could be adopted as their pre-match anthem.

"It was fantastic for us," he said, "and I was especially pleased that it happened when Roy was still alive. Can you imagine being asked if a song you had written could be sung by thousands in Scotland's biggest stadium before every home international?

"It gave Roy a tremendous feeling of pride and I'm sure he'd be delighted that it is still being sung today."

The song was first performed on a popular Scottish television programme in 1969 and Browne remembers it starting life in an archaic style, harping back to its story-time of great battles in Scotland's past where English armies were 'sent homeward tae think again.'

"We used to write songs and present them to each other and this was one of Roy's and I thought 'that's fine, let's get it in then'. But we were both surprised when it became so popular. It started on the circuit we played, and was taken to by our audiences, and then it started appearing in plays and on TV, often being sung by a Scots drunk!

"The first rugby link came in 1974 when Scottish players Billy Steele and Gordon Brown introduced it to the British and Irish Lions tour and it went down so well the squad adopted it as their tour anthem.

"We were just delighted to hear it being sung by supporters around the stadium and I still enjoy it when I go to games now."

When it was played at a funereal pace in Paris a few years ago, however, there was criticism that it was time for a change. In fact, more flak was directed at the local band which had mistaken the tempo, and a Scots pipe band duly flew out for the following French encounter and restored pride with a more rousing version.

O' Flower of Scotland has survived attempts to have it replaced with what critics suggest might be a more up-to-date, upbeat song, but whenever votes are called for it remains the choice of the passionate majority.

Many forget it is a modern folk song, recalling more a spirit and passion in the Scottish psyche as prevalent now as ever, than playing on any significant historical facts. In fact, when asked by the players if the anthem could be longer - in response to a lengthy Welsh anthem - Browne chose the third verse, which states of the English battles, that they 'are past now, and in the past they must remain', while urging Scots to still show their pride and passion.

Browne added: "There have been issues about it being too nationalistic, but it's a song, nothing more, and it has given lots of people enjoyment, which was, for Roy and myself, the very essence of The Corries' music.

"It has been chosen by Scottish rugby supporters and that says it all really."

By **DAVID FERGUSON** Chief rugby writer for *The Scotsman*

35 YEARS OF WATCHING SCOTLAND

BRIAN MEEK HAS BEEN COVERING SCOTLAND INTERNATIONALS FOR 35 YEARS, AN ODYSSEY THAT BEGAN AT LANSDOWNE ROAD IN DUBLIN

February 24, 1968 was the date of the first Scotland match I ever covered. Before the game, I was standing at the back of the grandstand when a complete stranger came up to me and declared: "We beat you last week and will do it again this time."

Puzzled by this assertion, because there had been no corresponding fixture the week before, I enquired what the fellow meant. "Celtic 3 Rangers 1" he triumphantly replied. This is not the strangest thing that ever happened to me at Erin's isle but it was a bizarre beginning. The guy was quite right by the way, as Ireland won 14 - 8 despite the best efforts of such players as Jock Turner, John Frame, Pringle Fisher and Alastair McHarg.

Anyway, I was new on the rota and in November saw Scotland beat Australia at Murrayfield – a rare event nowadays – before they went on to defeat France 6 - 3 at Colombes the following January. This was one of the most amazing victories as the home side had about 90 per cent of the chances, the English referee had to be rescued by the gendarmes and our captain Jim Telfer scored the winning try. Whatever happened to him?

There followed a fairly fallow period for Scottish successes though the South Africans were beaten by three points at a "fortress" Murrayfield in December 1969. Thousands of police had to ward off attempts by a large number of anti-apartheid demonstrators to invade the field. The police succeeded but it was hardly a happy occasion.

For me, the first real milestone has to be the match at Twickenham on March 20, 1971. Scotland had not won at the English HQ since before the Second World War and there was little indication of that statistic being altered. The Scots had lost their three previous championship matches and were hot favourites for the wooden spoon.

Yet with six Gala men in the side, they pulled off an astonishing 16 - 15 victory, captain Peter Brown converting Chris Rea's try with the final kick of the game. Grown men wept, and Brown wrote a new page in the history of the Scottish game. Gordon Brown and Jock Turner (two of the stalwarts of that team) are sadly no longer with us, but the memories linger on.

For the next 13 years Scotland produced a host of brilliant players, including Andy Irvine, Ian McLauchlan, Colin Telfer, Jim Renwick, Sandy Carmichael, David Leslie, Douglas Morgan, Ian McGeechan, Mike Biggar, Colin Deans, Keith Robertson and Alan Tomes. Many of these players went on to give sterling service to the British Lions, but there was no significant progress in achieving Championship, Triple Crown or Grand Slam successes.

The game was strictly amateur in those times with the SRU setting its face against any alteration to that status. Any player defecting to rugby league was effectively ostracised for the rest of his playing life.

Journalists were just about tolerated, if not exactly loved by the authorities. On a flight to Wales in the seventies, it was discovered the aircraft was overloaded. "Take off the press boys" ordered the Union President of the day and it was done.

To reach the press box at Murrayfield one had to pass through a gentlemen's toilet, which certainly did not encourage attendance by women reporters. Yet barriers were being lowered, thanks to men of vision like Wilson Shaw, Alec Brown, first coach Bill Dickinson and Jimmy Ross.

In 1984 Scotland suddenly moved up a gear, reaching heights which astonished many of us. A team coached by Jim Telfer, captained by another Borderer Jim Aitken, and containing only two players from non-Scottish clubs during the entire campaign, won all four Championship matches.

The side was built around half-backs John Rutherford and Roy Laidlaw, with Peter Dods as the most reliable goal kicker of his generation. Iain "The Bear" Milne and Aitken had Colin Deans between them in the front row, Jim Calder, Iain Paxton and David Leslie were the back three.

It was Leslie who destroyed Wales in Cardiff, while the centres David Johnston and Euan Kennedy carved up England. Laidlaw, as often before, saw off Ireland while Calder and Dods dished out the punishment to France. A Championship, Triple Crown, and Grand Slam had arrived and to be honest no one was entirely sure how to handle such success.

The next year Scotland lost all four Championship matches – 'from the Slam to the Slump' as one of our headline writers put it. But we had been there for the first time since 1925, so we knew it could be done again. Six years later, it was.

This was McGeechan's team, with David Sole in charge on the field. The Hastings brothers Gavin and Scott were at their peak, the adopted Kiwi Sean Lineen a vital ingredient, with Chick Chalmers and Gary Armstrong as the half-backs.

John Jeffrey and Finlay Calder were

the luminaries among the forwards, aided and abetted by "Del Boy" Cronin and Derek White plus hooker Kenny Milne. The 1990 Slam was most delicious for many because, on the final day of the Championship, the English were also going for the same prize.

Who could forget Tony Stanger fastening on to Gavin's kick and plunging over for the deciding try? Why, even shoppers in Jenners' store stopped to cheer the result.

Well, despite another Championship title, it has not been too thrilling for Scotland in the last decade. We have, as a rugby nation, struggled a bit in the professional era, and our domestic structure has been subject to much change and considerable controversy. It has become harder to compete against the top nations who have more money, better resources and more players than Scotland does. Yet I am neither despondent nor inclined to look back at the "good old days".

Today's players are fitter, and the game itself is faster and more entertaining to watch. A country of our size is never going to dominate world rugby but we can bring down the high and mighty from time to time.

When I first went to report rugby internationals I would wake up on a Saturday morning with a feeling of excitement in the pit of my stomach. I still do.

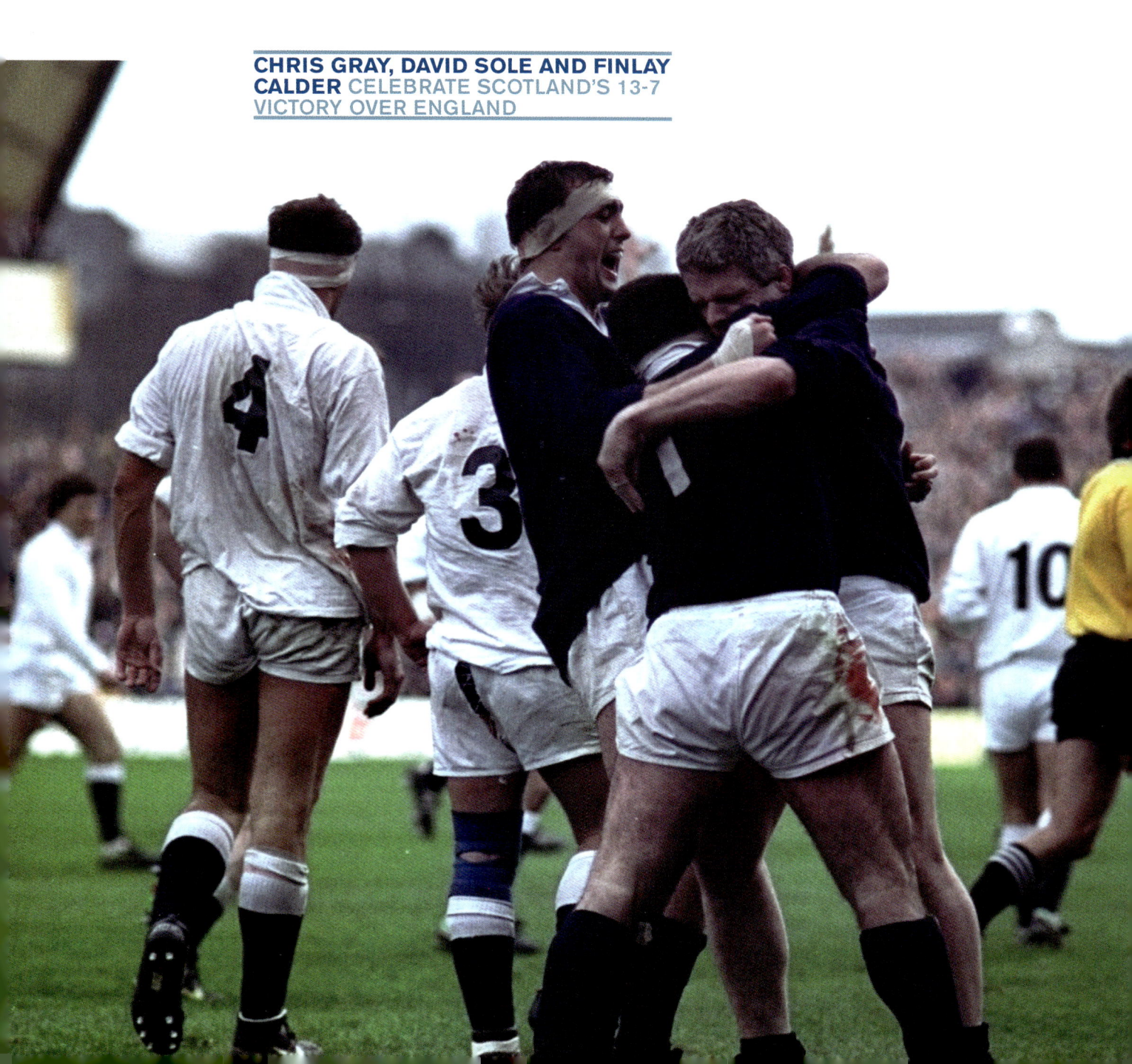

CHRIS GRAY, DAVID SOLE AND FINLAY CALDER CELEBRATE SCOTLAND'S 13-7 VICTORY OVER ENGLAND

MATCHDAY BUILD UP

MATCH DAY AT MURRAYFIELD

One of the most famous arenas in world sport, Murrayfield comes alive with 67,500 people on match day.

The waving scarves, hoisting of flags, exploding fireworks and sheer noise that reverberates around the Scottish stadium provides a colourful memory for all who attend international games. The countdown to the teams entering the lovingly-manicured field of play begins early in the morning, However, close to 2,000 people have work to do when Scotland entertain nations from around the world. Here, Kevin Ferrie takes a look at five of the busiest performers, those who feel the tension of international match day more than most and come into their own in the name of Scottish rugby.

THE PLAYER: GREGOR TOWNSEND

I used to sleep for as long as I could on match days, and would get up around 10.30, but now I like to eat as much as I can, so I have a proper breakfast at 8am.

Like a few players, I take a sleeping pill the night before to make sure I get at least eight hours, but between breakfast and lunch, at around 11, it's hard not to think about the game and what you want to do and the nerves kick in. I try to leave jobs for myself to do to take my mind off it, and after lunch I pack my bag, polish my boots, shower, listen to the TV and generally try to make the time go by quickly.

About 1.15 we meet up as a squad and jerseys are handed out and the coach, Ian McGeechan, tends to use the time more for motivational, sometimes emotional talks, rather than tactical stuff before we get on the bus. It's great seeing the supporters. We stopped at the gates to the stadium once and walked in behind a band, which was quite special, but usually we draw up at the players' tunnel and walk through the lines of supporters and into the dressing rooms. I tend to get in and try to relax, read through the programme, cards and messages we receive - I spend long enough on the pitch kicking and warming-up that I try not to rush out there.

We spend a good while warming up inside, beside the changing room, and after warming up as a team on the pitch, we come back in about ten minutes before kick-off, and, with the coaches now gone, the captain has the last few words of advice and encouragement. The referee calls us two minutes from kick-off and there is nothing to beat running out of the tunnel and hearing the Scottish crowd. The playing of 'Highland Cathedral' was a great innovation and it is some feeling as it reaches its crescendo and we get onto the field. What happens after that you all see for yourselves, but however it goes, good or bad, there is a proud feeling every time to be out on Murrayfield playing for Scotland.

GREGOR TOWNSEND I PACK MY BAG, POLISH MY BOOTS, SHOWER, LISTEN TO THE TV AND GENERALLY TRY TO MAKE THE TIME GO BY QUICKLY

By **KEVIN FERRIE** Chief rugby writer for *The Herald*

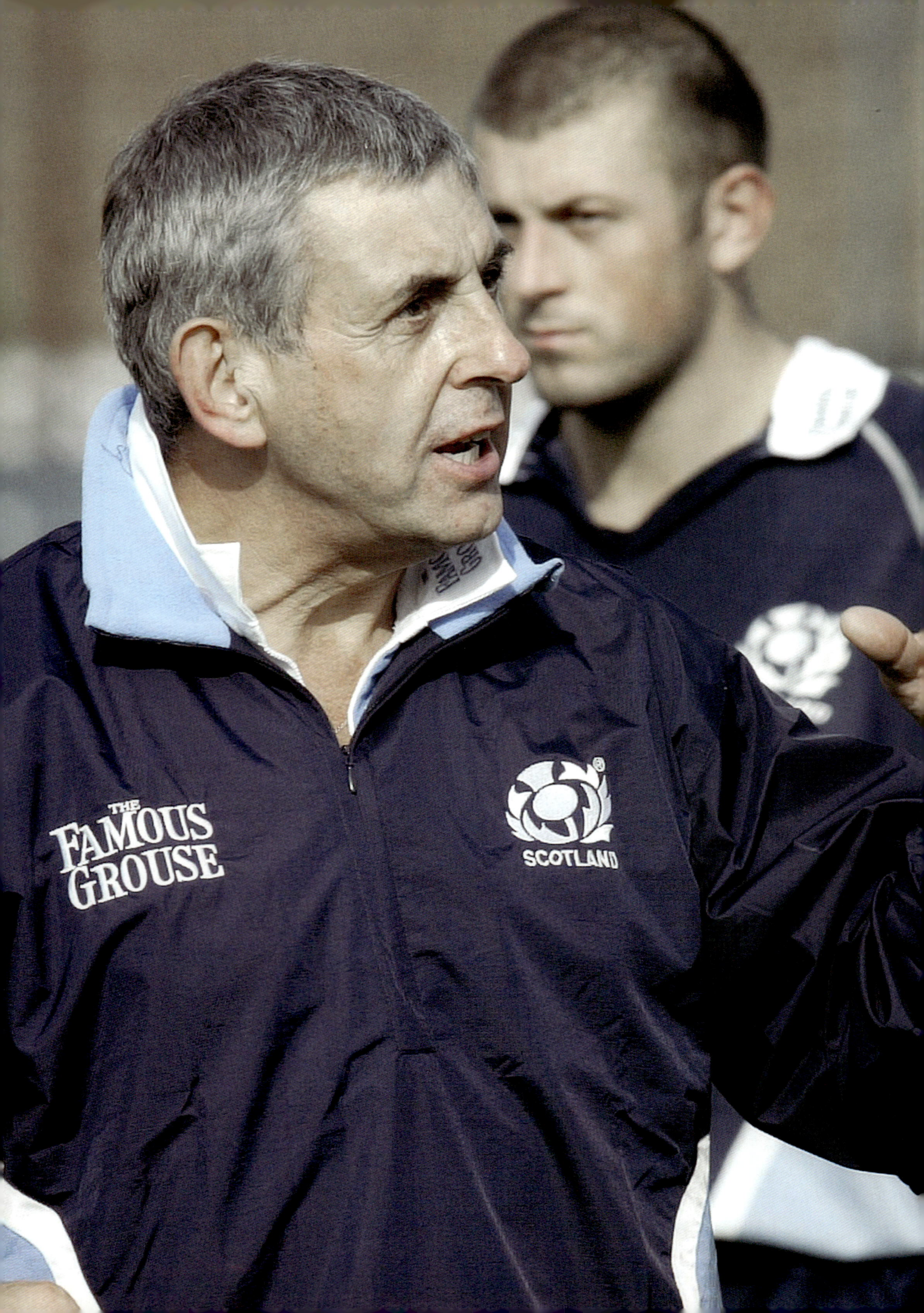
THE
FAMOUS
GROUSE
SCOTLAND

THE COACH: IAN MCGEECHAN

Everything's well planned for match day. I get up about 7.45am and have breakfast with a couple of players and the coaches, to talk through things.

The timings are all worked out, but it becomes very personal on match-day, and, while I'm doing things, I'll spend all morning with my team talk going through my mind. I still get very nervous on match-day, the same as when I was a player, and often I'll go for a quiet walk on my own to try and get my thoughts together. Then we have lunch and the whole mood changes.

Some people who haven't been close to a team won't fully understand, but it's almost like a switch has been flicked. It's right because you're trying to create a Test match animal, and an international player has a very strong competitive instinct which starts to come to the surface as we get nearer to the game. That's why it's hard to talk to players on match day, and I'm the same - not great to be around when the match is approaching, I'm afraid.

On the bus journey to Murrayfield, seeing supporters, you feel the occasion, and as you swing in to Murrayfield it's pretty obvious to everyone, me as well, that you're coming into an exclusive international environment. From the point we walk into the tunnel everything is meticulously planned to the last 30 seconds, and I like to make sure the players have the best possible support. I'll always go straight to the pitch and check the four corners, and have a few words with individuals. We'll go through the options from the kick-off, but you have to manage the dressing room - some players like a few words, some like to be left alone.

Once the game's underway, I'm into the detail and try to be quite objective, and make assessments of what's going well, what tactics have to be changed, which players have to do things differently, and I look at just three or four key points to bring out at half-time. We now have a managed programme for the three hours after the game, ensuring the players are properly rehabbed with the medics, and though I'm dealing with the media, trying to get round every player and then meeting the wives and girlfriends, I'm still liaising with the medics all the time.

I enjoy the dinner because you get the chance to relax, speak to opponents and coaches, but in the back of my mind there is always the game and how it went. As soon as I get home, I write down immediate thoughts on a couple of A4 sheets and then view the game on Sunday morning. By then I'm already thinking about what we have to change, how we build on the game and the focus has switched to the next one.

IAN MCGEECHAN I STILL GET VERY NERVOUS ON MATCH-DAY, THE SAME AS WHEN I WAS A PLAYER, AND OFTEN I'LL GO FOR A QUIET WALK ON MY OWN TO TRY AND GET MY THOUGHTS TOGETHER

THE EVENTS MANAGER: ALLAN SNEDDEN

I'm at the stadium before 8am if it's a 3pm kick-off, for a walk round the stadium with the police, checking security and safety, particularly if the weather has been bad.

Then it's time for the entertainment rehearsals, which can involve dancers, pipe bands, singers and mini rugby teams, they rehearse to make sure they all know where they should be and when and we check the PA and sound systems and make sure that it all sounds great.

It's hard to please 67,500 people every time, but I think the entertainment has helped make the internationals a great family day out, even if does give us more work. We must liase with parachutists and the weather centre, for example, to find out if they can jump, and because they're based in Auchterarder we have to make a call on that no later than 90 minutes before they are due in the stadium.

Four hours before kick-off, car park attendants, turnstile staff, merchandise sellers and catering staff all arrive and are kitted out with security passes, two-and-a-half hours before kick-off, all vehicle movement in the stadium stops, and two hours before kick-off the turnstiles open and we're off.

The entertainment from that moment on is all geared to build towards kick-off - the teams coming out of the tunnel is the cork coming out of the champagne bottle, with all the pre-match build-up creating the bubbly atmosphere. Another reason for the entertainment is to try and change the Scottish culture where around 70% of our supporters arrive at the game in the half-hour before kick-off, which creates severe congestion problems. It is changing, though, and more are coming earlier now.

I spend the first half sorting late arrivals, wrong seats etc, and I tend to see maybe 20 minutes of the game in the second half before the final whistle sounds and it goes nuts again.

My team are now in charge of organising the post-match dinner and that means we're on until 10.30pm, and after that I usually go into town to meet some friends - who invariably have had a few beers already - and then go home with incredibly sore feet. It's a hard day, but great to be part of.

ALLAN SNEDDEN: IT'S HARD TO PLEASE 67,500 PEOPLE EVERY TIME, BUT I THINK THE ENTERTAINMENT HAS HELPED MAKE THE INTERNATIONALS A GREAT FAMILY DAY OUT

THE KIT MANAGER: DAVID ROMPREY

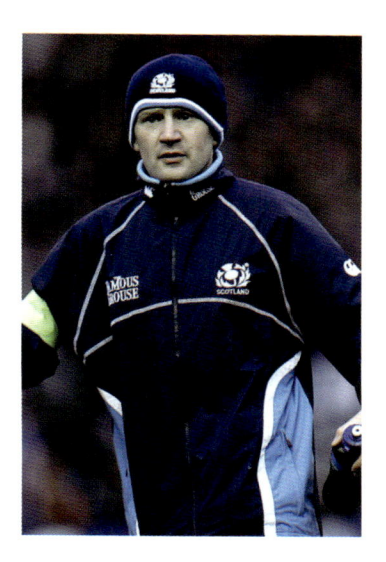

DAVID ROMPREY I ALWAYS FEEL A SENSE OF PRIDE THAT I'M PART OF THIS

My day starts at 9am, with me laying out the jerseys and sticking up the name-plates on the right pegs - the players choose themselves where they sit and you get used to their preferences. They get one set of kit, with a second jersey for debutants only, so they can keep their first one and swap the other, and once it's all out - if you mix up Bryan Redpath's size 36 shorts with Mattie Stewart's 44s there will be trouble - I check the balls, making sure the pressure is right in the training balls for both teams and the six match balls. I fill the ice baths, ice machines and water bottles, drinks for drugs tests and post the day's timetable in the dressing rooms, refs' and medical rooms. A radio message after 1pm tells me of the players arrival and I open the doors. I have water ready for them, some go straight to the pitch, others sit and read programmes, others get rubs and strapping, and then Alan Tait and I get balls, cones and tackle bags out for the warm-up. This is when you get requests for tea and coffee, new studs and laces, and, once, a new gum-shield - I've got everything! I get butterflies, especially when you see the guys in there, pouring water over their heads, banging their chests or the walls, and the aggression builds. When I see the focus and determination of Gordon Bulloch or Gregor Townsend as they come into the tunnel I always feel a sense of pride that I'm part of this. During the game I help with water, at half-time pass out drinks and am basically on hand to help anyone that needs me afterwards. My full-time job is looking after the kit - which goes right from under-18s, to under-19s, under-21s, women's, A, sevens, seniors, refs, development officers, the lot - but we all help each other on match days. There is a great team spirit right through the whole set-up and though the blood is at boiling point when it's game time, we stick together and work hard to help the team. It can be tough, but you do feel it's a privilege to be there playing a part.

THE HEAD GROUNDSKEEPER: HEATHER MACKINNON

Match day is usually the chaotic end to a long week. In the lead-up we'll work till 7.30pm most nights and later on the night before, and I'll be in by 7am on match-day itself. The first job is to give the pitch its final roll, to firm it up and bring the presentation up. Four of us go out and roll it across the way.

Sometimes there are people rehearsing entertainment or TV checks being done and we're asked to switch off machines, so often we're rushing against the clock. We finish off the line marking - we'll have done most of it on Friday - with the two touchlines and five and ten-metre lines, using string lines and boards to ensure it's all very precise. Then someone is tasked to go out and check the bolts through the crossbar are tight, just in case, and we get the posts padded up, the flags in, the sand buckets out for the kickers, mark in a blue line across which the press can't go and make sure The Famous Grouse birds, Sammy and Joey, are in place on trackside.

I always feel a bit anxious until that point, but then we can relax a bit usually. Once, before the Barbarians match, one of the guys put a flag in and it went through an undersoil heating pipe. Water started spurting out, so we had to lift the turf, repair the pipe, repair the hole and put it all back in place, which we did before anyone noticed, I think! When the game's on we sit in behind the Scotland dug-out, and go out and repair marks at half-time, which can be fun when mini-rugby players are running at you, or performers dancing around.

Sometimes, for the entertainment, they put the lights out, so we're left roaming around in the dark filling in divots! Ground staff are placed on the four corners before the final whistle so we can get on and get the pads and flags before supporters, and once the teams are off we get out and try to repair the pitch. Like helping the players recover quickly, it's best to get out quickly after the game and help the pitch recover. If you get an overnight frost, it can seriously damage exposed areas, so we work on the pitch for a couple of hours. I don't tend to go out celebrating afterwards because I'm so tired after a hectic week - going home for a beer and a Chinese meal is my perfect finish!

26 PORTRAITS OF REDPATH

PORTRAITS OF BRYAN REDPATH - THE SCOTLAND SKIPPER REPRESENTED IN THE EYES OF HIS CHILDREN

Bryan Redpath at home with his wife Gill and children Amy, Cameron and Murray.

"I LOVE DAD" BY **AMY REDPATH**

"MY DADDY" BY **CAMERON REDPATH**

LEARNING FROM THE SCOTS - A SASSENACH'S VIEW FROM JOHN SCOTT, CAPTAIN OF ENGLAND WHEN SCOTLAND BEAT THEM AT TWICKENHAM FOR ONLY THE SECOND TIME IN 45 YEARS

There are many images that flash through my mind when I'm asked about my memories of Scottish rugby but one stands out more than any other. Not a match, not a place, not even an incident – but one strapping, heroic player in dark blue who represented all that was best about the game not only north of the border but anywhere that rugby is played.

IAIN PAXTON AND **TOM SMITH** OF SCOTLAND JUMP IN A LINE OUT AGAINST STEVE BAINBRIDGE OF ENGLAND AT TWICKENHAM. SCOTLAND WON THE GAME 15-12

I'm thinking, of course, of Gordon Brown. For me he really was one of 'the greatest'. I can't adequately put into words what exactly he had that made him so special, apart from his obvious integrity and respect for everyone he came into contact with, but whatever it was I just wish we could bottle it and pass on to all our young players today. But I have to say that it wasn't a peculiarly Scottish thing, more a case of the man himself. Two other all-time greats out of the same mould would have to be Willie-John McBride and Fran Cotton.

That's enough of the compliments, for the moment at least. Here am I, an English forward who played five times against the pride of Scotland, won the first three, and the last two…well, let's just say my recollections are a bit hazy about those. First of all there were the good times. My first ever game against Scotland was in fact a schools' international at Galashiels in 1973 which we won 27-9. Five years later my first senior caps were against France and Wales and then we came up to Murrayfield for the Calcutta Cup match.

I quickly learned that playing against Scotland was totally different to anything that had gone before. At that time the Welsh match was always regarded as the toughest one for obvious reasons, not least because Gareth Edwards, Gerald Davies and the rest of their superstars were in their prime. But Scotland? Well, they 'only' had Andy Irvine, Jim Renwick, Colin Deans and Mighty Mouse!

GARETH CHILCOTT SAID "ALL ENGLAND HAVE TO DO IS TO TURN UP." AS **MATT DAWSON** FOUND TO HIS COST. CHILCOTT WAS WRONG

ROB ANDREW, TONY STANGER, JEREMY GUSCOTT AND JOHN JEFFREY IN ACTION DURING SCOTLAND'S 1990 GRAND SLAM VICTORY

Looking at these names it's hard to believe that in my era there was a feeling that the Scottish game was the one we least worried about. We should have known better. Admittedly those first three Calcutta Cup matches for me were victories, but always at a price.

Take 1980 – a glorious Grand Slam on paper. The final score of 30-18 looks great in the record books but it certainly doesn't tell the full story. In many ways it was a strange occasion. We went off like a bomb at the start and built up a big lead. That was just as well because the points cushion saved us as Scotland grew stronger the longer that the game went on. The final whistle couldn't come soon enough and England finished as triumphant heroes – but it was never that easy.

We won again the following year but in 1983 Scotland brought us down to earth with a bang. We should have won our opening game in Cardiff with something to spare but allowed Wales back into the game for a draw. Then the captaincy passed to me. It was a time of transition in English rugby and there was a lot of muddled thinking. It was an honour for me to be captain when there were other notable candidates like Peter Wheeler still in the team.

But I soon realised that I was the figurehead of a team that did not gel together and Scotland made us pay for it. We lost the Calcutta Cup match 12-22 – only our second defeat to Scotland at Twickenham in 45 years. Things didn't get any better a year later when we lost again at Murrayfield. By then I had long since learned that any Scotland side is formidable simply because the sum is greater than the parts.

I don't mean that in any detrimental way. It seems to me that in Scotland you've always had one thing spot on in that the pinnacle of the game is the international side. Of course there is a need for a strong club structure week-in, week-out, but the shop window, and the yardstick by which everything and everyone in rugby is measured, is the success of the national side. And no one can doubt that whether winning or losing every Scotland side had a distinctive style. They seem to be coached in the fine arts of the game, almost purist in form, and every now and again an outstanding team is the reward.

The result is that every so often a high-flying English team gets ambushed at Murrayfield – ask Will Carling about the joys of the Grand Slam that never was in 1990, while 10 years later Matt Dawson found himself in a similar situation. Like myself all those years before they can take consolation in the knowledge that a right going-over by a Scottish pack is a vital part of their rugby education. Well, that's our excuse, anyway.

It's generally believed that Scotland has taken longer than the other European countries to embrace professionalism in all its forms. I'm not entirely sure that is the case, as many other countries have considerable progress to make. I would argue that in Scotland the idea that local clubs should be strictly amateur and embrace the traditions of 'rugger' as of old is no bad thing. The game has always been well taught in your schools as well as the clubs and whatever the fortunes of the new professional teams in Edinburgh, Glasgow and the Borders I sincerely hope that the Hawicks, Galas and Boroughmuirs of this world survive long into the future.

What would be really interesting is an international side in the present-day Six Nations that is locked in a time warp. By that I mean a team that was born out of a purely amateur set-up, but still with its quota of class players, imbued with the old values of the game and competing against professional teams.

The smart money would be on such a team doing at least as well as the countries that have been propping up the final table in recent years. And where better to try out such an experiment than in Scotland. In such a time warp the only possible captain would be Gordon Brown.

TOM SMITH - SCOTLAND'S DYNAMIC PROP

KEVIN FERRIE CONSIDERS THE EFFECTS THAT PROFESSIONALISM HAS HAD ON THE SCOTLAND TEAM

It was all right for rugby league back in 1895. All they had to do was create a different version of the sport when the row over broken time payments erupted. A century on with the opportunity that time had provided for the development of so many traditions and cultures, turning rugby union professional was always going to be a much more complex business.

SCOTT MURRAY NOW PLAYS HIS RUGBY FOR EDINBURGH. OTHER PLAYERS WHO HAVE RETURNED TO SCOTLAND INCLUDE: GREGOR TOWNSEND, GARY ARMSTRONG AND DODDIE WEIR

So it has proven. Admittedly in the southern hemisphere where the sport was already virtually professional, and to a lesser extent France, the transition was relatively smooth. In the countries where the sport began, however, the set in their ways Home Unions, turmoil has reigned.

Particularly so, it seemed, in Scotland. Whereas strong club cultures in England and Wales and a tradition of well supported Inter-Provincial rugby in Ireland meant it seemed relatively easy for them to find a way forward, Scotland was torn.

Clubs with support bases in tiny Border towns or former pupil communities did not have the potential to develop as the English and Welsh might. The districts, meanwhile, played a handful of matches each year usually in front of even fewer spectators than the top clubs. However the benefit of that was that the issues had to be confronted early and they were, with many casualties on the way.

The old SRU had to be overhauled with more of the decision making being handled by full-time professionals rather than amateur committee men. Professional teams were set up with ways found of coaxing many players and coaches away from good professional careers and mistakes were made, most particularly in reducing from four to two. That those two were initially referred to as "superteams" when they struggled to beat anyone merely added to the feeling that Scottish rugby was something of a laughing stock in the wider rugby world. Leading players like Tom Smith and Stuart Grimes felt they had to leave. Others like Gregor Townsend, Scott Murray, Gary Armstrong and Doddie Weir took a long time to decide to return home.

Who is laughing now, though? While professionalism has helped the Irish they were still, as the 2002/03 season began, struggling to find a way of appeasing clubs who still felt they should see more of their leading players. In Wales the problems were much, much worse, with debate raging over whether they should move from an emphasis on clubs at the top level to introducing a professional set up.

Meanwhile Scottish rugby remains a sport that relies on a tiny percentage of participants in the sport from what is an already small population. This means its major successes will remain relatively few and far between, just as it has been during a century of Five and Six Nations competition which produced a total of three Grand Slams.

Yet sometimes it can be 'good tae see ourselves as others see us,' as our bard suggested and not only for the soul. Consequently the words of Gareth Jenkins, the highly popular coach of Llanelli the most consistent Celtic outfit in the history of the European Cup alone in never having had a losing record in the pool stages and twice having reached the semi-finals were encouraging.

"They have got the right coaching structure and player environment in place and we just haven't moved on," he said.

"It is a question of structure of the sides up there. I am the only full-time professional coach at Llanelli and it all comes down to the way things are organised and the funding to do things the right way.

"We are playing international sides with international quality players. People have to understand that and accept it. We have no divine right to beat these sides but they have made tremendous strides in Scotland in the way everything is organised there."

Tremendous strides indeed, but as that statement was made Scotland's professionals had, in seven years of professional rugby, still won just two championships, becoming Five Nations Champions in 1999 and winning the Culcutta Cup trophy in 2000, while neither Edinburgh nor Glasgow had reached the quarter-finals in the European Cup before the Borders came on stream.

That said, the professional game remains in its infancy and much can still be done to improve the system, but Scottish rugby at least seems to have got past the worst.

By **KEVIN FERRIE** Chief rugby writer for *The Herald*

SCOTLAND

2

GORDON BULLOCH

Position Hooker	The player who has made the biggest impact on my rugby career Gary Armstrong
Date of Birth 26 March 1975	The most exciting game I have ever played in was France v Scotland, Paris 1999
Height 5ft 11in	Other than the Scotland coach, the coach I would most like to play under would be Dave Barrett - likes the laid back approach
Weight 15st 12lb	Apart from Scotland, who I would put my money on to win the next World Cup Australia
International Points 20 - 4t	In the Rugby World Cup final the team I would least like as the other finalist would be Australia
Club Glasgow	
Caps 44	

PLAYER PROFILE

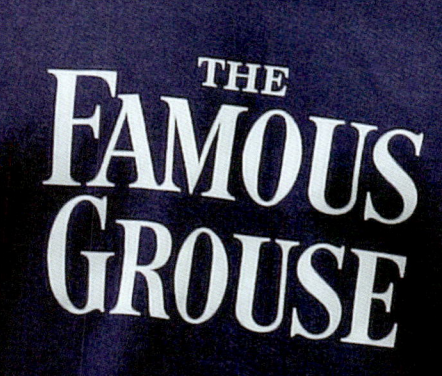

BULLOCH
HOOKER

SCOTLAND

BRUCE DOUGLAS

3

Position
Prop

Date of Birth
10 Febuary 1980

Height
5ft 11in

Weight
17st 10lb

International Points
-

Club
Glasgow

Caps
3

The player who has made the biggest impact on my rugby career
Jocky Bryce

The most exciting game I have ever played in was
Scotland v South Africa 2002

Other than the Scotland coach, the coach I would most like to play under would be
Tony Gilbert

Apart from Scotland, who I would put my money on to win the next World Cup
France

In the Rugby World Cup final the team I would least like as the other finalist would be
New Zealand

PLAYER PROFILE

DOUGLAS
PROP

SCOTLAND

STUART GRIMES

5

Position
Lock

Date of Birth
4 April 1974

Height
6ft 5in

Weight
17st

International Points
15 - 3t

Club
Newcastle Falcons

Caps
44

The player who has made the biggest impact on my rugby career
David McIvor

The most exciting game I have ever played in was
France v Scotland '99, Tetley Bitter Cup Final 2001

Other than the Scotland coach, the coach I would most like to play under would be
Dougie Morgan

Apart from Scotland, who I would put my money on to win the next World Cup
Australia

In the Rugby World Cup final the team I would least like as the other finalist would be
Australia

PLAYER PROFILE

GRIMES
LOCK

SCOTLAND

5

NATHAN HINES

Position
Lock

Date of Birth
29 November 1976

Height
6ft 7in

Weight
18st 5lb

International Points
5 - 1t

Club
Edinburgh

Caps
6

The player who has made the biggest impact on my rugby career
Todd Blackadder

The most exciting game I have ever played in was
Northampton v Edinburgh, Heineken Cup

Other than the Scotland coach, the coach I would most like to play under would be
Graham Hogg

Apart from Scotland, who I would put my money on to win the next World Cup
France

In the Rugby World Cup final the team I would least like as the other finalist would be
Doesn't matter, if we're good enough to make it, we're good enough to win it

PLAYER PROFILE

HINES

LOCK

SCOTLAND 3

DAVID HILTON

Position
Prop

Date of Birth
3 April 1970

Height
5ft 10in

Weight
16st

International Points
5 - 1t

Club
Glasgow

Caps
43

The player who has made the biggest impact on my rugby career
-

The most exciting game I have ever played in was
France v Scotland 1999

Other than the Scotland coach, the coach I would most like to play under would be
Jim Telfer

Apart from Scotland, who I would put my money on to win the next World Cup
Australia

In the Rugby World Cup final the team I would least like as the other finalist would be
Australia

PLAYER PROFILE

HILTON
PROP

MARTIN LESLIE

SCOTLAND — 7

Position
Back Row

Date of Birth
25 October 1971

Height
6ft 3in

Weight
16st 7lb

International Points
50 - 10t

Club
Edinburgh

Caps
29

The player who has made the biggest impact on my rugby career
Graeme Burns

The most exciting game I have ever played in was
France 1999

Other than the Scotland coach, the coach I would most like to play under would be
Bobby Bonami

Apart from Scotland, who I would put my money on to win the next World Cup
New Zealand

In the Rugby World Cup final the team I would least like as the other finalist would be
England

PLAYER PROFILE

LESLIE
BACK ROW

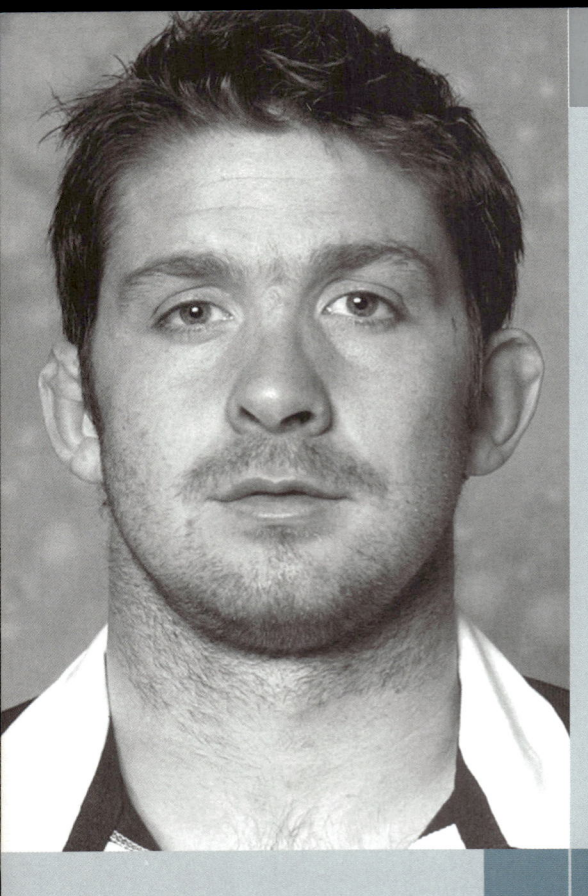

SCOTT MURRAY

4

SCOTLAND

Position
Lock

Date of Birth
15 January 1976

Height
6ft 6in

Weight
16st 8lb

International Points
10 - 2t

Club
Edinburgh

Caps
42

The player who has made the biggest impact on my rugby career
Willie Patterson (Prestonlodge)

The most exciting game I have ever played in was
England 2000

Other than the Scotland coach, the coach I would most like to play under would be
Rudolf Struaeli

Apart from Scotland, who I would put my money on to win the next World Cup
New Zealand

In the Rugby World Cup final the team I would least like as the other finalist would be
New Zealand

PLAYER PROFILE

MURRAY
LOCK

SCOTLAND

JON PETRIE

8

Position Back row	The player who has made the biggest impact on my rugby career **Andy Nicol**
Date of Birth 19 October 1976	The most exciting game I have ever played in was **28-28 draw against Wales at Murrayfield**
Height 6ft 4in	Other than the Scotland coach, the coach I would most like to play under would be **Rod MacQueen**
Weight 17st 2lb	Apart from Scotland, who I would put my money on to win the next World Cup **Australia**
International Points 5 - 1t	In the Rugby World Cup final the team I would least like as the other finalist would be **Australia**
Club Glasgow	
Caps 15	

PLAYER PROFILE

PETRIE
BACK ROW

BUDGE POUNTNEY

SCOTLAND 7

Position
Flanker

Date of Birth
13 November 1973

Height
6ft

Weight
14st 7lb

International Points
25 - 5t

Club
Northampton Saints

Caps
31

The player who has made the biggest impact on my rugby career
Garry Pagel

The most exciting game I have ever played in was
Scotland v England 2000 and Northampton v Munster Heineken Cup Final

Other than the Scotland coach, the coach I would most like to play under would be
Wayne Smith

Apart from Scotland, who I would put my money on to win the next World Cup
New Zealand

In the Rugby World Cup final the team I would least like as the other finalist would be
New Zealand

PLAYER PROFILE

POUNTNEY
FLANKER

SCOTLAND

TOM SMITH

1

Position
Prop

Date of Birth
31 October 1971

Height
5ft 11in

Weight
15st 7lb

International Points
25 - 5t

Club
Northampton Saints

Caps
40

The player who has made the biggest impact on my rugby career
Too many to mention

The most exciting game I have ever played in was
England 2000 Six Nations

Other than the Scotland coach, the coach I would most like to play under would be
Rod MacQueen

Apart from Scotland, who I would put my money on to win the next World Cup
New Zealand

In the Rugby World Cup final the team I would least like as the other finalist would be
Australia

PLAYER PROFILE

SMITH

PROP

SCOTLAND

SIMON TAYLOR

6

Position
Back row

Date of Birth
17 August 1979

Height
6ft 4in

Weight
16st 7lb

International Points
5 - 1t

Club
Edinburgh

Caps
16

The player who has made the biggest impact on my rugby career
Zinzan Brooke

The most exciting game I have ever played in was
Sotland v South Africa 2002

Other than the Scotland coach, the coach I would most like to play under would be
Bertie Vogts

Apart from Scotland, who I would put my money on to win the next World Cup
New Zealand

In the rugby World Cup final the team I would least like as the other finalist would be
New Zealand

PLAYER PROFILE

TAYLOR
BACK ROW

SCOTLAND

2

STEVE SCOTT

Position
Hooker

Date of Birth
26 July 1973

Height
6ft

Weight
17st

International Points
-

Club
The Borders

Caps
9

The player who has made the biggest impact on my rugby career
Todd Blackadder

The most exciting game I have ever played in was
Scotland A v Italy A 2002

Other than the Scotland coach, the coach I would most like to play under would be
Jim Telfer

Apart from Scotland, who I would put my money on to win the next World Cup
Australia

In the Rugby World Cup final the team I would least like as the other finalist would be
Australia

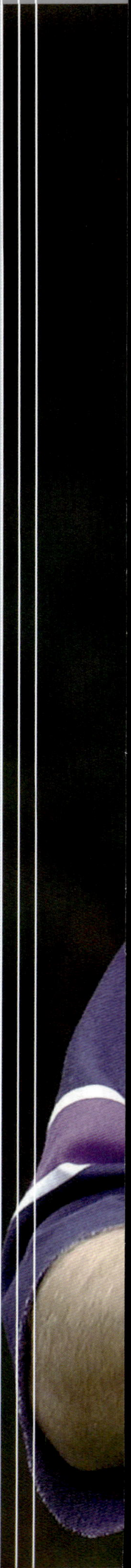

PLAYER PROFILE

SCOTT
HOOKER

SCOTLAND

JASON WHITE

4

Position
Lock

Date of Birth
17 April 1978

Height
6ft 5in

Weight
18st

International Points
5 - 1t

Club
Glasgow

Caps
20

The player who has made the biggest impact on my rugby career
Stuart Grimes

The most exciting game I have ever played in was
Scotland v England 2000

Other than the Scotland coach, the coach I would most like to play under would be
David Leslie

Apart from Scotland, who I would put my money on to win the next World Cup
France

In the Rugby World Cup final the team I would least like as the other finalist would be
Australia

PLAYER PROFILE

WHITE
LOCK

GRAEME BEVERIDGE

SCOTLAND 9

Position
Scrum half

Date of Birth
17 February 1976

Height
5ft 6in

Weight
12st 9lb

International Points
-

Club
Glasgow

Caps
4

The player who has made the biggest impact on my rugby career
Gordon Wilson with his fighting spirit

The most exciting game I have ever played in was
Scotland Students v Japan 1996 World Cup S.A Final score 60 - 40

Other than the Scotland coach, the coach I would most like to play under would be
Sean Lineen and Rod MacQueen

Apart from Scotland, who I would put my money on to win the next World Cup
Australia

In the Rugby World Cup final the team I would least like as the other finalist would be
Who cares as long as we're in it

PLAYER PROFILE

BEVERIDGE
SCRUM HALF

SCOTLAND 13

ANDY CRAIG

Position
Centre

Date of Birth
16 March 1976

Height
6ft 1in

Weight
14st 8lb

International Points
5 - 1t

Club
Orrell

Caps
5

The player who has made the biggest impact on my rugby career
Ellery Hanley and Jason Robinson

The most exciting game I have ever played in was
Scotland v South Africa 2002

Other than the Scotland coach, the coach I would most like to play under would be
John Mitchell

Apart from Scotland, who I would put my money on to win the next World Cup
Australia or France

In the Rugby World Cup final the team I would least like as the other finalist would be
Australia

PLAYER PROFILE

CRAIG
CENTRE

SCOTLAND 15

BEN HINSHELWOOD

Position	The player who has made the biggest impact on my rugby career
Centre	I have to say my old man!
Date of Birth	The most exciting game I have ever played in was
22 March 1977	Scotland v South Africa '02 (21-6) I only played 10 minutes but I was the most excited I have ever been on a rugby pitch
Height	
6ft 3in	
	Other than the Scotland coach, the coach I would most like to play under would be Worcester coach Andy Keast, very good technician
Weight	
15st 7lb	
International Points	Apart from Scotland, who I would put my money on to win the next World Cup
-	New Zealand
Club	In the Rugby World Cup final the team I would least like as the other finalist would be
Worcester	New Zealand
Caps	
4	

PLAYER PROFILE

HINSHELWOOD
CENTRE

SCOTLAND 15

BRENDAN LANEY

Position
Full back/Centre

Date of Birth
16 November 1973

Height
6ft

Weight
15st

International Points
111 - 2t 16c 23p

Club
Edinburgh

Caps
11

The player who has made the biggest impact on my rugby career
A club mate in Temuka - Steve Tarrant

The most exciting game I have ever played in was
3rd extra time club match semi final at home (New Zealand)

Other than the Scotland coach, the coach I would most like to play under would be
Tony Gilbert/Laurie Mains

Apart from Scotland, who I would put my money on to win the next World Cup
New Zealand

In the Rugby World Cup final the team I would least like as the other finalist would be
Anyone, just as long as we win

PLAYER PROFILE

LANEY
FULL BACK

SCOTLAND 15

STUART MOFFAT

Position
Full back/Wing

Date of Birth
18 August 1977

Height
6ft 3in

Weight
15st 7lb

International Points
5 - 1t

Club
Glasgow

Caps
3

The player who has made the biggest impact on my rugby career
Gavin Hastings

The most exciting game I have ever played in was
Scotland v South Africa 2002

Other than the Scotland coach, the coach I would most like to play under would be
Ian Milward

Apart from Scotland, who I would put my money on to win the next World Cup
Australia

In the Rugby World Cup final the team I would least like as the other finalist would be
Australia

PLAYER PROFILE

MOFFAT
FULL BACK

SCOTLAND

11

CHRIS PATERSON

Position
Wing/Stand-off

Date of Birth
30 March 1978

Height
6ft

Weight
12st 5lb

International Points
59 - 7t 6p 3c

Club
Edinburgh

Caps
25

The player who has made the biggest impact on my rugby career
Todd Blackadder

The most exciting game I have ever played in was
Scotland v England

Other than the Scotland coach, the coach I would most like to play under would be
Jim Telfer

Apart from Scotland, who I would put my money on to win the next World Cup
New Zealand

In the Rugby World Cup final the team I would least like as the other finalist would be
Australia

PLAYER PROFILE

PATERSON

WING

SCOTLAND

BRYAN REDPATH

9

Position
Scrum half

Date of Birth
2 July 1971

Height
5ft 7in

Weight
12st 5lb

International Points
5 - 1t

Club
Sale Sharks

Caps
48

The player who has made the biggest impact on my rugby career
No player but Jim Telfer has had a big impact

The most exciting game I have ever played in was
Scotland v France 1995

Other than the Scotland coach, the coach I would most like to play under would be
Jim Telfer

Apart from Scotland, who I would put my money on to win the next World Cup
France

In the Rugby World Cup final the team I would least like as the other finalist would be
If we got to the final I wouldn't mind

PLAYER PROFILE

REDPATH
SCRUM HALF

SCOTLAND 10

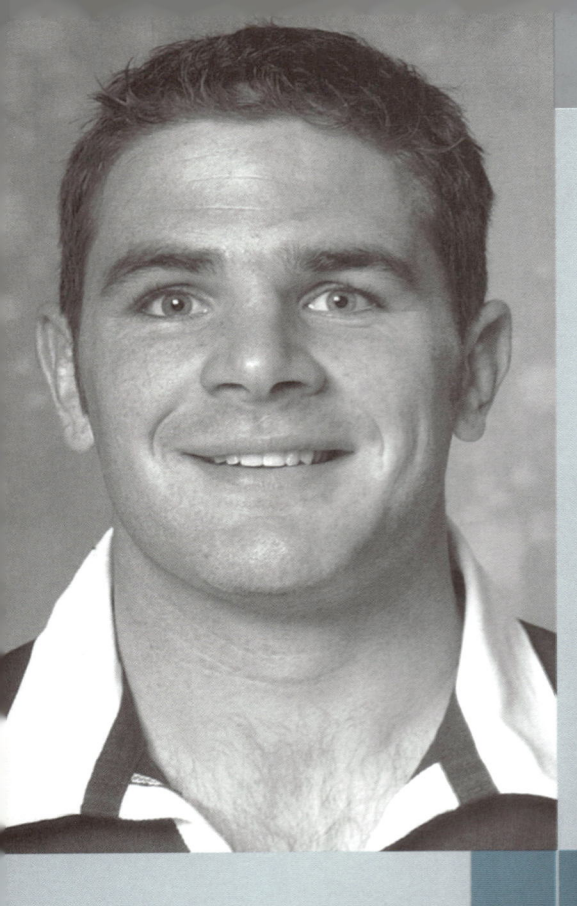

GORDON ROSS

Position	Stand-off
Date of Birth	8 March 1978
Height	5ft 8in
Weight	12st 10lb
International Points	23 - 5p 3c
Club	Leeds Tykes
Caps	4

The player who has made the biggest impact on my rugby career
Gregor Lawson

The most exciting game I have ever played in was
Scotland u'19 v England u'19, 1997

Other than the Scotland coach, the coach I would most like to play under would be
Graham Hogg

Apart from Scotland, who I would put my money on to win the next World Cup
New Zealand

In the Rugby World Cup final the team I would least like as the other finalist would be
New Zealand

PLAYER PROFILE

ROSS
STAND-OFF

GREGOR TOWNSEND

Position
Stand-off/Centre

Date of Birth
26 April 1973

Height
6ft

Weight
14st 5lb

International Points
157 - 16t 14p 7c 7dg

Club
The Borders

Caps
69

The player who has made the biggest impact on my rugby career
Stephen Larkham

The most exciting game I have ever played in was
France v Scotland 1995

Other than the Scotland coach, the coach I would most like to play under would be
Wayne Smith

Apart from Scotland, who I would put my money on to win the next World Cup
France

In the Rugby World Cup final the team I would least like as the other finalist would be
New Zealand

PLAYER PROFILE

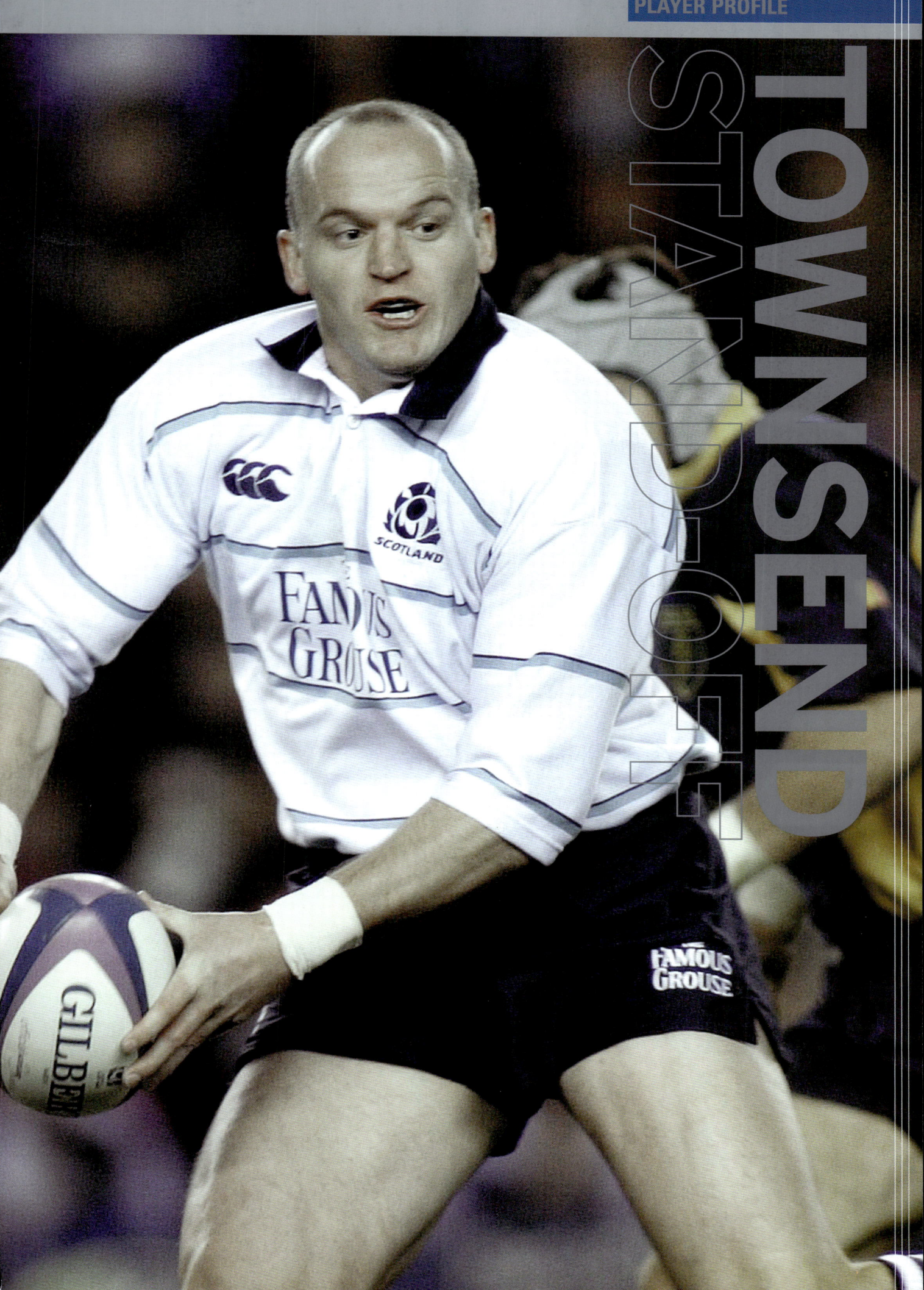

TOWNSEND
STAND-OFF

SCOTLAND 14

NIKKI WALKER

Position	
Wing	The player who has made the biggest impact on my rugby career
	Richard Metcalfe
Date of Birth	
5 March 1982	The most exciting game I have ever played in was
	Hawick v Glasgow Hawks cup final 2002
Height	
6ft 4in	Other than the Scotland coach, the coach I would most like to play under would be
	Tony Gilbert
Weight	
15st	Apart from Scotland, who I would put my money on to win the next World Cup
	France
International Points	
5 - 1t	In the Rugby World Cup final the team I would least like as the other finalist would be
	Australia
Club	
The Borders	
Caps	
3	

PLAYER PROFILE

WALKER
WING

ACKNOWLEDGEMENTS

Scottish Rugby Union
Laura Laidlaw — *Marketing Manager, Scotland Brand*
Julie Pearson — *Marketing Officer, Scotland Brand*
Fiona White — *Library Services Manger*
Graham Law — *Head of Media and PR*
Sarah Niblock — *Media and PR Officer*

GreenPark Publishing
Peter Francomb — *Publishing Director*
Rod Hobbs — *Creative Director*
Martin Jenkins — *Senior Designer*
George Roberts — *Sub Editor*
Paul Hobbs — *Advertising Manager*

Contributors
Todd Blackadder — *Edinburgh Rugby*
Alan Evans — *Cardiff RFC*
Kevin Ferrie — *The Herald*
David Ferguson — *The Scotsman*
David Kelso — *Kelvin Media*
Alan Lorimer — *The Herald*
Bill Lothian — *Edinburgh Evening News*
George Mackay — *The Mail on Sunday*
Bill McMurtrie — *Glasgow District Administrative Executive*
David MacGregor — *BBC Radio*
Brian Meek — *The Herald*
Norman Mair
Frank Moran — *Sunday Telegraph*
Grant Robbins
John Scott — *England No. 8 (1978-1984)*
Alan Shaw — *The Sunday Post*

Photography
Gordon Fraser — *SRU Official Photographer*
Simon Safferey — *Simon Saffery Photography*
Allsport